AMERICAN FEAST

COOKBOOKS AND COCKTAILS

from the Library of Congress

Fruit and wine on table, circa 1880. Chromolithograph. Prints and Photographs Division.

AMERICAN FEAST
COOKBOOKS AND COCKTAILS
from the Library of Congress

By Zach Klitzman and Susan Reyburn

Foreword by Carla D. Hayden,
Librarian of Congress

Washington, DC

© 2023 Library of Congress

ISBN 978-0-8444-9583-5

Library of Congress Cataloging-in-Publication Data

Names: Klitzman, Zach, author. | Reyburn, Susan, author. | Hayden, Carla Diane, 1952- writer of foreword.

Title: American feast : cookbooks and cocktails from the Library of Congress / by Zach Klitzman, Susan Reyburn ; foreword by Carla D. Hayden.

Description: Washington, DC : Library of Congress, [2023] | Series: Collection close-up | Includes index. |

Identifiers: LCCN 2022055227 | ISBN 9780844495835 (paperback)

Subjects: LCSH: Cookbooks--United States--History. | Cocktails--United States--History. | Food writing--United States--History. | Food--Social aspects--United States. | Library of Congress--Catalogs.

Classification: LCC TX644 .K55 2023 | DDC 641.3009--dc23/eng/20221117

LC record available at https://lccn.loc.gov/2022055227

JUNE 2023

Menu

Foreword

THE LIBRARY OF CONGRESS—THE LARGEST LIBRARY IN THE WORLD—HOLDS MILLIONS OF BOOKS IN HUNDREDS OF LANGUAGES, AND TENS OF THOUSANDS OF THEM ARE RELATED TO FOOD AND DRINK. WHETHER YOU WANT TO MAKE JULIA CHILD'S BEEF BOURGUIGNON OR STIR UP A HORSE'S NECK COCKTAIL, YOU WILL FIND THOSE RECIPES IN OUR COLLECTIONS.

Among its culinary treasures, the Library has a fifteenth-century cookbook manuscript, *Libro de arte coquinaria*, along with the earliest printed cookbook, *De honesta voluptate & valetudine* (1480). Other rare items include "Manner of Cookery," a Japanese block book from 1642; Hannah Glasse's *Art of Cookery Made Plain and Easy* (1747), the bestselling cookbook of the eighteenth century in England and the American colonies; *American Cookery* (1796) by Amelia Simmons, the first cookbook written by an American and published in the United States; and the first-ever mention of a cocktail from a New Hampshire newspaper in 1803.

American cookbooks have mirrored the nation's growth in size, scope, and diversity. New immigrant populations, arriving en masse during the nineteenth century, introduced an array of cuisines and accompanying cookbooks. Recipes for beverages also grew in cultural relevance parallel to the development of American cookbooks. These cookbooks offer key insights into what people eat, how they prepare it and share that knowledge, and what kinds of events demand certain dishes. They also tell us how tastes, expectations, and kitchen technology evolve over time.

The items featured in *American Feast: Cookbooks and Cocktails from the Library of Congress* have been selected from a variety of the Library's collections, including the Prints and Photographs Division; the Rare Book and Special Collections Division; the Manuscript Division; the Veterans History Project; the Motion Picture, Broadcasting, and Recorded Sound Division; and the Science, Technology, and Business Division, where most of the Library's cookbooks are held. They represent significant facets of American cookery, from handwritten recipes passed down across generations to huge compendiums of recipes for every possible occasion.

The Library of Congress has a wealth of appetizing culinary treasures, whether you are a gourmet chef or don't know your spritzes from your bitters. I invite you to sample the other exciting tidbits in our Collection Close-Up series, and to visit in person or online at www.loc.gov.

Carla D. Hayden
Librarian of Congress

AMERICAN COOKE

OR THE ART OF DRESSING

VIANDS, FISH, POULTRY and VEGETABLES,

AND THE BEST MODES OF MAKING

PASTES, PUFFS, PIES, TARTS, PUDDINGS, CUSTARDS AND PRESERVES,

AND ALL KINDS OF

C A K E S,

FROM THE IMPERIAL PLUMB TO PLAIN CAKE.

ADAPTED TO THIS COUNTRY,

AND ALL GRADES OF LIFE.

By Amelia Simmons,

AN AMERICAN ORPHAN.

PUBLISHED ACCORDING TO ACT OF CONGRESS.

HARTFORD:

PRINTED BY HUDSON & GOODWIN,

FOR THE AUTHOR.

1796.

American Cookery

 Amelia Simmons

Hartford: Printed by Hudson & Goodwin for the Author

 1796

 Rare Book and Special Collections

CHAPTER 1

The Art of Dressing Viands"

EARLY AMERICAN COOKBOOKS AND COCKTAILS

What is the American feast? Perhaps its most salient feature is that it is constantly evolving, the nation's long history of immigration, migration, assimilation, and regionalization pushing it in new and different ways. American cooks, whether children just learning the craft or celebrity chefs demonstrating their art to millions on television, use human ingenuity and their inherent drive to experiment when cooking. As cookbook editor Judith Jones observed, "nothing is created out of whole cloth; each wave of immigrants . . . brought the tastes and techniques they grew up on in their native lands and adapted them to what they found here." One of her authors, Southern chef Bill Neal, put it thusly: "Our food tells us where we came from and who we have become."

In colonial America, cookbooks from Great Britain often were imported. Standards like Hannah Glasse's *The Art of Cookery* were popular throughout the thirteen colonies in wealthy white households (Martha Washington owned a copy). But without the exact same ingredients available as in the British Isles, early American cooks had to adapt and experiment to create their own interpretations.

"Other creatures receive food simply as fodder. But we take the raw materials of the earth and work with them—touch them, manipulate them, taste them, glory in their heady smells and colors, and then, through a bit of alchemy, transform them into delicious creations."

| **Cookbook editor**
Judith Jones

The first cookbook published by an American appeared twenty years after independence: *American Cookery* by Amelia Simmons. This publication transformed American cookbooks by recording recipes that used ingredients native to North America. The book's success immediately led to dozens of pirated, unauthorized editions. These early American cookbooks—whether wholly original or imitations—provided medical, sanitary, and household recipes in addition to those for food.

At the same time, enslaved cooks or poor white families often did not have access to printed cookbooks, in part because they did not have the opportunity to learn to read. Instead, they passed down recipes orally or occasionally dictated recipes to those who could transcribe them in recipe notebooks.

The first appearance and first definition of "cocktail" came in American newspapers in 1803 and 1806, respectively. Though contemporary cocktails can include just about any mixed drink involving liquor, in this period, a cocktail consisted of spirits, sugar, water, and bitters. Early American cocktails were more or less the precursor to the modern drink known, appropriately, as an "Old Fashioned."

Mary Coates's Book

 Mary Coates
(active 18th century)

 1740

Marian S. Carson Collection,
Rare Book and Special
Collections Division

A generation before the American
Revolution, colonist Mary Coates kept
this handwritten book of food recipes
and medicinal home remedies. The
recipes, in no particular order, fall
under straightforward headings (A
Good Recipe for a Cough and Another
Very Good Recipe for a Cough). Her
gingerbread recipe was among the
variations circulating in the colonies.

With a history dating back to ancient Greece, gingerbread
in medieval Europe was well established as traditional
Christmas cake and a standard treatment for nausea. Colonial
gingerbread recipes drew on British and German sources,
but Americans developed a more cake-like texture for their
gingerbread by incorporating potash as a leavening agent.

American Cookery, *or The Art of Dressing Viands, Fish, Poultry, and Vegetables: And the Best Modes of Making Pastes, Puffs, Pies, Tarts, Puddings, Custards, and Preserves: And All Kinds of Cakes, from the Imperial Plumb to Plain Cake, Adapted to this Country, and All Grades of Life.*

Amelia Simmons

Hartford: Printed by Hudson & Goodwin for the Author

1796

Rare Book and Special Collections Division

This cookbook is considered the first of American authorship to be printed in the United States. It also introduced new terms to American cuisine. Amelia Simmons used "slapjack" to describe a pancake recipe, creating a new version of flapjacks that remained popular in the eighteenth century.

She wrote the Dutch word *koekje* as "cookey," which led to the modern word "cookie," and *sla* became the modern slaw, as in a salad. Pictured here is the first recipe for a johnnycake. Simmons adapted traditional dishes by including ingredients native to North America, such as corn and squash. Her recipe for Pumpkin Pudding, baked in a crust, is the basis for the classic American pumpkin pie. Though *American Cookery* was widely available at the time as well as widely copied, only four original first edition copies, including the one shown here, still exist. It paved the way for American homegrown cookbooks, announcing that British cookbooks no longer were the only sources of English-language recipes.

Little is known about Simmons. She is described on the title page as "An American Orphan," and, while not illiterate, an advertisement for the second edition of the book stated that she lacked "an education sufficient to prepare the work for the press" without outside assistance. One theory posits that the book was written by "Amelia Simons" of Windham, Connecticut, who was born in 1767 and died in November 1796, seven months after *American Cookery* was copyrighted. It is also possible that "Amelia Simmons" was a pseudonym, the use of which was common for eighteenth-century publications.

JOURNAL.

FRIDAY.—Waked at 7 by the bell—wonder what people mean by disturbing one so early after an Assembly: turn'd and doz'd 'till 9 : got up, and dressed—felt queer ; took a cup of coffee—no appetite.——10. Lounged to the Doctor's—found Peter--talked of the girls—smoked half a cigar—felt rather squally: Van Hogan came in—quiz'd me for looking dull—great bore.——11. Drank a glass of cocktail—excellent for the head ; all sauntered away to see the girls : Miss —— not up : Went to the Squire's—girls just done breakfast. *Mem.* Girls not so bright after dancing. Talked of the weather—then of the walking—then of the weather again—was very witty—Peter not quite so brilliant. Went to the Col's. found the girls very lively and sociable—drank a glass of wine—talk'd about Indians—call'd Miss —— a Squaw—all laugh'd—damn'd good one—talked about the walking—insisted that the more muddy it was, the better walking—all look'd queer : nothing else to say—jogg'd off. Call'd at the Doct's. found Burnham—he looked very wise—drank another glass of cocktail. All went to the Printing Office—began to smoke—Mons. —— look'd into an old paper—stupid fellow—never look into papers my-

"Journal," Farmer's Cabinet

 Amherst, NH

 April 28, 1803

Newspaper & Current Periodical Division

The first printed use of the word "cocktail" appeared in a humorous first-person account published in the New Hampshire newspaper *Farmer's Cabinet* on April 28, 1803. "Drank a glass of cocktail—excellent for the head," the anonymous diarist wrote. This drink was the third attempted stimulant of the day; earlier he had drunk a cup of coffee and tried a cigar, but neither made him feel better. Clearly the cocktail worked, since after drinking it he "sauntered away to see the girls."

Letter to the editor and reply, The Balance, and Columbian Repository

Letter author unknown; reply by Harry Croswell (1778–1858)

Hudson, NY

May 13, 1806

Newspaper & Current Periodical Division

On May 6, 1806, Harry Croswell wrote in his Federalist newspaper *The Balance, and Columbian Repository* that a Democratic candidate for the New York legislature had bought rum, brandy, gin, bitters and "25 do[ses] cocktail" to ply potential voters (as was common at the time), yet had lost the election. An anonymous reader sent in a letter asking for the definition of "this precious species of refreshment," and in the May 13 edition, Croswell provided the pictured response: "*Cock-tail*, then, is a stimulating liquor, composed of *spirits* of any kind, *sugar*, *water*, and *bitters*." A hyperpartisan editor, he also got a dig in at his opposition: a cocktail "is said also to be of great use to a democratic candidate: because a person having swallowed a glass of it is ready to swallow anything else."

New American Cookery, or

Female Companion. Containing Full and Ample Directions for Roasting, Broiling, Stewing, Hashing, Boiling, Preserving, Pickling, Potting, Fricasees, Soups, Puff-Pastes, Puddings, Custards, Pies, Tarts, &c. Also, the Making of Wines and Cheese. Peculiarly Adapted to the American Mode of Cooking.

 "By an American Lady"

 New York: T.B. Jansen

 1805

 Katherine Golden Bitting Collection on Gastronomy, Rare Book and Special Collections Division

64

in every other ingredient except the plumbs, which work in when going into the oven.

Independence Cake.

Twenty pound flour, 15 pound sugar, 10 pound butter, 4 dozen eggs, one quart wine, 1 quart brandy, one ounce nutmeg, cinnamon, cloves, mace, of each 3 ounces, two pound citron, currants and raisins 5 pound each, 1 quart yeast; when baked, frost with loaf sugar; dress with box and gold leaf.

Buckwheat Cakes.

One quart buckwheat flour, 1 pint of milk or new beer, 3 spoons molasses, 4 do. yeast, stir well together, wet the bottom of the pan with butter or lard, and when the pan is hot, put in the cakes, when done, pour over butter and milk.

Federal Pan Cake.

Take one quart of boulted rye flour,

Early American cookbooks frequently reprinted recipes from previously published cookbooks without attribution. Amelia Simmons's *American Cookery* was reprinted in four plagiarized versions, including the 1805 *New American Cookery* shown here. New recipes added to the plagiarized versions subsequently appeared in authorized editions, muddying the provenance of individual recipes. The recipes for Election Cake, Independence Cake, and Federal Pan Cake depicted here appeared in several editions. Calling for large quantities, they indicate the role that food played in early American political life, where rallies supplied sustenance both literal and metaphorical to the politically engaged.

Drawing of a Macaroni Machine and Instructions for Making Pasta

 Thomas Jefferson
(1743–1826)

 ca. 1787

 Thomas Jefferson Papers, Manuscript Division

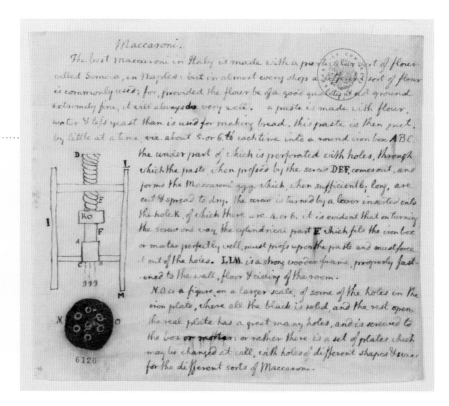

The third president of the United States, Thomas Jefferson, acquired a taste for European cooking while serving as American minister to France in the 1780s. Jefferson brought his enslaved attendant, James Hemings, with him to train as a chef there. When they returned home in 1790, they brought many recipes from French, Italian, and other European cuisines, including a precursor to what are now called French fries. Jefferson served rare European wines, and he was one of the first Americans to serve delicacies like ice cream, peach flambé, and macaroons. Macaroni, with or without helpings of cheese, was another culinary fascination for Jefferson. He drew this diagram of a pasta machine, complete with holes showing how the dough can be extruded, and drafted a macaroni recipe, likely dictated by a chef or butler, on the back. Jefferson often served macaroni pie in the White House, a novelty that sometimes delighted and sometimes confused fellow politicians, such as Representative Manasseh Cutler, who said the dish "tasted very strong, and not agreeable."

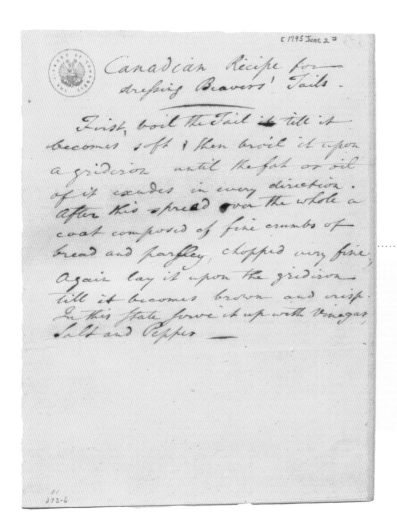

E 1795 June 2]

Canadian Recipe for dressing Beavers' Tails.

First, boil the Tail till it becomes soft & then broil it upon a gridiron until the fat or oil of it exudes in every direction. After this spread over the whole a coat composed of fine crumbs of bread and parsley, chopped very fine; Again lay it upon the gridiron till it becomes brown and crisp. In this State serve it up with Vinegar Salt and Pepper —

Canadian Recipe for Dressing Beavers' Tails

 George Turner (ca. 1750–1845)

 June 2, 1795

George Washington Papers, Manuscript Division

Among the most unusual items in the papers of George Washington is a letter Judge George Turner sent from Cincinnati, in which he presents the president with a buffalo robe adorned with porcupine quills as well as a dozen beaver tails and the depicted recipe to cook the latter. This Canadian specialty involves boiling, broiling, and grilling the tails, which exude a delicious fat similar to bone marrow. It is unknown whether the president actually cooked or ate such delicacies.

Enslaved Chefs

THOUGH GEORGE WASHINGTON AND THOMAS JEFFERSON RECEIVED UNREQUESTED RECIPES AND BROUGHT CULINARY TREATS FROM EUROPE TO AMERICA, THEY WERE NOT THE ONES DOING THE COOKING. IN FACT, ONE ENSLAVED BLACKSMITH AT MONTICELLO, ISAAC GRANGER JEFFERSON, STATED THAT THE ONLY TIME JEFFERSON EVER ENTERED THE KITCHEN WAS TO WIND THE TALL CASE CLOCK INSTALLED THERE. INSTEAD, ENSLAVED COOKS PREPARED THE FOOD IN WASHINGTON AND JEFFERSON'S HOMES.

Hercules Posey (1748–1812) cooked for Washington while he was president. Enslaved to Washington's neighbor, Posey had been legally transferred to Washington in 1767 to settle a debt, and by 1786 he was listed as the cook at Mount Vernon. In 1790, he moved to Philadelphia with Washington, who was serving as president there. He received permission for his son Richmond to work in the kitchen with him, and he earned income by selling leftovers from the kitchen. George Washington Parke Custis, the president's step-grandson, described Posey as "a celebrated artiste" who was "as highly accomplished [and] proficient in the culinary art as could be found in the United States." On Washington's birthday in 1797, Posey self-emancipated, perhaps because he had been forced to work as a bricklayer and gardener at Mount Vernon instead of as a chef. Washington's attempts to capture Posey failed. Posey most likely died in New York City in 1812.

Jefferson inherited **James Hemings (1765–1801)** through his marriage to Martha Wayles—though Hemings was also Martha's half-brother. At the age of 19, Hemings accompanied Jefferson to France, where in 1785 he began his culinary training. One of his teachers cooked for the prince de Conde, Louis XIV's great-grandson. Upon returning to America, Hemings continued as a chef, receiving the same pay as Jefferson's white household staff. It is likely that he helped introduce or refine the recipe for ice cream, though credit has often been attributed to Jefferson's French butler, Petit. In 1793, Jefferson promised Hemings his freedom as long as he trained someone to take over his cooking duties, and in 1796 he received that freedom after training his brother Peter. After manumission he traveled, eventually working in a Baltimore tavern in 1801. At that time, Jefferson asked through intermediaries for him to cook at the White House. Hemings wanted a direct offer from Jefferson but never got it; the president hired a native French chef instead. Hemings, who likely suffered from alcoholism, committed suicide that fall.

The Universal Receipt Book,

or Complete Family Directory: Being a Repository of Useful Knowledge in the Several Branches of Domestic Economy; Containing Scarce, Curious, and Valuable Receipts, and Choice Secrets / By a Society of Gentlemen in New-York

Richard Alsop (1761–1815)

New York: Published by I. Riley
Van Winkle & Wiley, printers

1814

Katherine Golden Bitting Collection on Gastronomy, Rare Book and Special Collections Division

A collection of expensive and occasionally exotic recipes, this receipt (an alternative form of "recipe") book was the work of one industrious man, Connecticut writer-naturalist-bibliophile-tinkerer Richard Alsop, rather than the collective effort its title suggested. Alsop ranged far beyond meal recipes, offering a full complement of restoratives for health (as in his "lozenges for the heart burn," shown here),

home repair, and handy household items, such as grease stain remover and ink. Many entries were likely his own creations. His "Cure for a Felon—Said to Be Certain," which calls for rock salt, butter nut, and a green cabbage leaf, might suggest a startlingly efficient crime prevention method but for the fact that "felon" in Alsop's day also referred to a small abscess or inflamed sore, which, though not as threatening to society at large, usually demanded quick attention as well.

Maria Eliza Ketelby Rundell (1745–1828)

 New York: Johnstone & Van Norden

 1823

 Katherine Golden Bitting Collection on Gastronomy, Rare Book and Special Collections Division

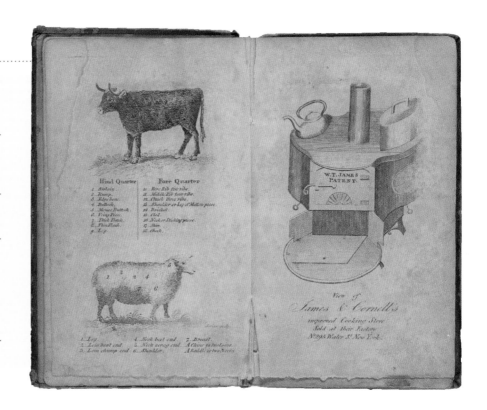

The Experienced American Housekeeper, *or Domestic*
Cookery, Formed on Principles of Economy for the Use of Private Families

Although Maria Rundell, a comfortably well-off mother of five, was an experienced collector of recipes and sensible advice, the British lady was not an American, experienced or otherwise. Hailing from Shropshire and frequenting London, Bath, and the continent, she published *A New System of Domestic Cookery* (1806) anonymously—as was often the case then with female authors—through a family friend. Riddled with unapproved editorial changes and exasperating typographic errors, the book embarrassed its author, and Rundell demanded her publisher produce a corrected edition. For this 1823 American edition, New York editors Yankee-Doodled up the title and inserted new recipes to appeal to a stateside audience. The book was a mainstay in middle-class American and British kitchens for generations, remaining in print into the late nineteenth century.

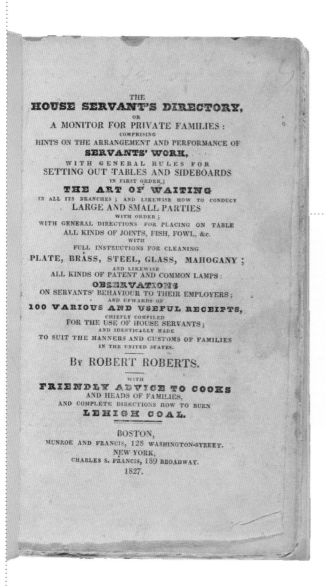

THE

HOUSE SERVANT'S DIRECTORY,

OR

A MONITOR FOR PRIVATE FAMILIES:

COMPRISING

HINTS ON THE ARRANGEMENT AND PERFORMANCE OF

SERVANTS' WORK,

WITH GENERAL RULES FOR

SETTING OUT TABLES AND SIDEBOARDS

IN FIRST ORDER;

THE ART OF WAITING

IN ALL ITS BRANCHES ; AND LIKEWISE HOW TO CONDUCT

LARGE AND SMALL PARTIES

WITH ORDER ;

WITH GENERAL DIRECTIONS FOR PLACING ON TABLE

ALL KINDS OF JOINTS, FISH, FOWL, &c.

WITH

FULL INSTRUCTIONS FOR CLEANING

PLATE, BRASS, STEEL, GLASS, MAHOGANY ;

AND LIKEWISE

ALL KINDS OF PATENT AND COMMON LAMPS :

OBSERVATIONS

ON SERVANTS' BEHAVIOUR TO THEIR EMPLOYERS ;

AND UPWARDS OF

100 VARIOUS AND USEFUL RECEIPTS,

CHIEFLY COMPILED

FOR THE USE OF HOUSE SERVANTS ;

AND IDENTICALLY MADE

TO SUIT THE MANNERS AND CUSTOMS OF FAMILIES

IN THE UNITED STATES.

By ROBERT ROBERTS.

WITH

FRIENDLY ADVICE TO COOKS

AND HEADS OF FAMILIES,

AND COMPLETE DIRECTIONS HOW TO BURN

LEHIGH COAL.

BOSTON,

MUNROE AND FRANCIS, 128 WASHINGTON-STREET.

NEW YORK,

CHARLES S. FRANCIS, 189 BROADWAY.

1827.

The House Servant's Directory, *or A Monitor for Private Families*

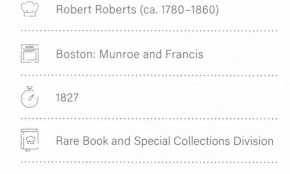

Robert Roberts (ca. 1780–1860)

Boston: Munroe and Francis

1827

Rare Book and Special Collections Division

This book is one of the first to be written by an African American and widely published. Robert Roberts worked for Christopher Gore, a former US senator and governor of Massachusetts, who hosted guests such as Daniel Webster and James Monroe in his Waltham mansion. Based on Roberts's observations of daily life as the household manager, the book was aimed at chefs, butlers, and other servants of the wealthy, not an average home cook. Though there are some recipes for food, most of the publication focuses on running a household, with instructions for setting tables, sharpening knives, building coal fires, and cleaning furniture. Roberts's book made its way around the country; Andrew Jackson owned a copy at his Tennessee home, the Hermitage.

The Frugal Housewife:
Dedicated to Those Who Are Not Ashamed of Economy

 Lydia Maria Child (1802–1880)

 Boston: Marsh & Capen, and Carter & Hendee

1829

 Katherine Golden Bitting Collection on Gastronomy, Rare Book and Special Collections Division

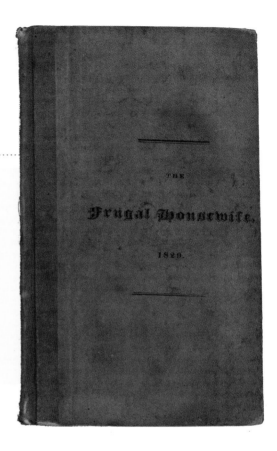

In her introduction to *The Frugal Housewife*, reformer and writer Lydia Maria Child made clear just who her intended audience was: "Books of this kind have usually been written for the wealthy: I have written for the poor!" Believing that economical household hints were missing from existing cookbooks, she wrote hers "to teach how money can be *saved* not how it can be *enjoyed*." With chapter titles such as "Odd Scraps for the Economical," "Simple Remedies," "Cheap Dye Stuffs," and "Cheap Common Cooking," she provided advice to make foodstuffs, household items, and medical remedies last longer and require less upkeep. Though the concept of "leftovers" as a discrete food category did not come about until the early twentieth century, Child nonetheless believed that "nothing should be thrown away so long as it is possible to make any use of it, however trifling that use may be." Despite a tone bordering on sanctimonious parsimony, the book supplanted *American Cookery* as the most popular cookbook of the day, going through more than thirty printings. Starting in 1832, editions included the word "American" in the title, to avoid confusion with British author Susannah Carter's 1765 book of the same name (though Child included a note in these editions deriding Carter's work as "not adapted to the wants of this country").

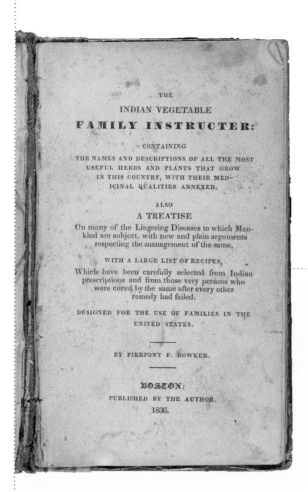

The Indian Vegetable Family Instructer:
Containing the Names and Descriptions of All the Most Useful Herbs and Plants That Grow in This Country, with Their Medicinal Qualities Annexed: Also a Treatise on Many of the Lingering Diseases to Which Mankind are Subject ... With a Large List of Recipes, Which Have Been Carefully Selected from Indian Prescriptions ... Designed for the Use of Families in the United States.

 Pierpont F. Bowker

 Boston: Published by the author

 1836

Marian S. Carson Collection, Rare Book and Special Collections Division

This little-known author, having "endeavored to state the true nature and virtue of each vegetable" turned to unnamed American Indian sources for finding relief "from obstinate diseases, which baffled the skill of the most eminent physicians." Pierpont Bowker sought to provide readers "a book whereby they may become their own physicians," having gone to considerable personal expense in its research and self-publication. His effort was, he claimed, no less "than universal philanthropy to mankind . . . a jewel of unprecedented worth." The book includes 182 descriptions of vegetables and herbs, one original ode to spring, one scorching essay on "Man's Ignorance of Medical Knowledge," and 156 recipes for treating maladies such as the king's evil, hysterics, rheumatism, piles, rickets, and worms, as well as the common cold.

Life Preserver. *John Weik's (Philadelphia) Kochbuecher [Cookbooks]*

 J. Nissle

 Lithograph

 ca. 1856

 Prints and Photographs Division

More than one million Germans immigrated to the United States in the aftermath of the failed German revolutions of 1848 and 1849. This wave peaked with 215,000 immigrants in 1854, just two years before this advertisement for German-American cookbooks was published. The immigrants brought their own recipes, culinary heritage, and cookbooks. As this detailed lithograph advertises, several German cookbooks soon entered the market, some solely in German and some bilingual. John Weik published the books advertised here, from authors Marianne Struf and William Vollmer. The intricate border scenes, showing farming, fishing, hunting, cooking, and eating, link the cookbooks with idyllic scenes of food preparation and consumption.

JOHN WEIK'S
(PHILADELPHIA)

KOCHBÜCHER [COOKBOOKS]

Wm. VOLLMER'S
Vollständiges deutsches
VEREINIGTE STAATEN
KOCHBUCH
Gebunden für 50 Cents

Wm. VOLLMER'S
Vollständiges Englisch Deutsches
VEREINIGTE STAATEN
KOCHBUCH
Gebunden für $1,00

Wm. VOLLMER'S
Complete
UNITED STATES COOKBOOK
Bound 50 Cents

MARIANNE STRÜF'S
Vollständiges
KOCHBUCH
für alle Stände
MIT ILLUSTRATIONEN
Gebunden $1,00

MARIANNE STRÜF'S
WIRTHSCHAFTLICHES
HAUSBUCH
FÜR STADT U. LAND
2 THEILE IN 1 BANDE.
Gebunden $1,00

ALLE FÜNF BÜCHER HIER ZU HABEN

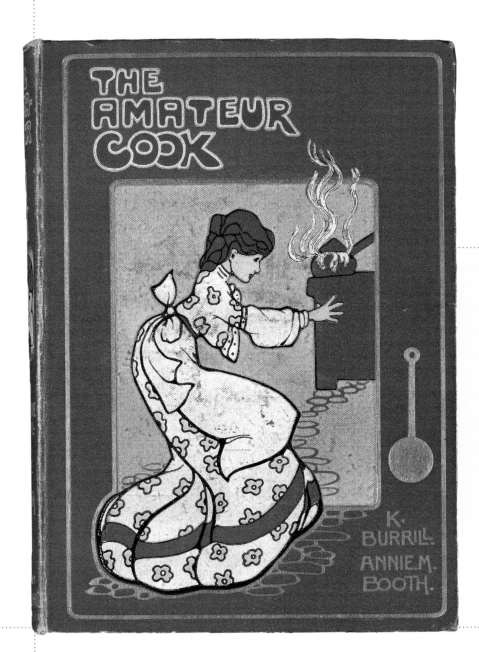

The Amateur Cook

 Katharine Burrill and
Annie M. Booth

 New York: F. A. Stokes

 1906

 Katherine Golden
Bitting Collection on
Gastronomy, Rare
Book and Special
Collections Division

CHAPTER 2

Condensed Scientific Knowledge"

NEW STANDARDS FOR FOOD AND DRINK

In the second half of the nineteenth century, American cookbooks expanded in scope, attractiveness, and diversity of content. Improvements in printing technology enabled the creation of beautiful covers as well as interior illustrations that showcased finished recipes or diagrammed specific instructions. Visual flourishes also were used to advertise cookbooks, and corporations marketed products such as kitchen appliances and ingredient staples via recipe cards, pamphlets, and cookbooks. Cookbooks included more recipes from a variety of ethnic cuisines, as new immigrants continued to arrive. Cookbooks written for children also appeared, and sales of community cookbooks raised funds for local charitable causes. Around the turn of the twentieth century, advances in American industry allowed for mass production of standardized cooking equipment, ingredients, and measurements, resulting in recipes that were more consistent. Popular cookbooks such as *The Boston Cooking School Cook Book* (1896) promoted the use of standard measurements to ensure this consistency.

Cocktails also became more standardized in this period, in part thanks to Jerry Thomas, a legendary bartender who wrote the first drinks recipe book in 1862. The book became a mainstay of cocktail culture for decades and was reissued in several different editions.

repeat till all is covered, leaving the meat in brine from four to seven weeks, according to size.

To PREVENT SKIPPERS IN HAM.—In order to avoid the skipper, and all worms and bugs that usually infest and destroy bacon, keep your smoke house *dark*, and the moth that deposits the eggs will never enter it. Smoke with green hickory, this is important, as the flavor of the bacon is often destroyed by smoking with improper wood.

METHOD OF CURING BAD BUTTER.—Melt the butter in hot water, skim it off as clean as possible, and work it over again in a churn, add salt and fine sugar, and press well.

To CLARIFY MOLASSES.—To free molasses from its sharp taste, and to render it fit to be used, instead of sugar, take twelve pounds of molasses, twelve pounds of water, and three pounds of charcoal, coarsely pulverized, mix them in a kettle, and boil the whole over a slow wood fire. When the mixture has boiled half an hour, pour it into a flat vessel, in order that the charcoal may subside to the bottom, then pour off the liquid, and place it over the fire once more, that the superfious water may evaporate, and the molasses be brought to their former consistence. Twelve pounds of molasses will produce twelve pounds of syrup.

SUBSTITUTE FOR CREAM IN TEA OR COFFEE.—Beat the white of an egg to a froth, put to it a very small lump of butter, and mix well, then turn the coffee to it gradually, so that it may not curdle. If perfectly done it will be an excellent substitute for cream. For tea omit the butter, using only the egg.

SUBSTITUTE FOR COFFEE.—Take sound ripe acorns, wash them while in the shell, dry them, and parch until they open, take the shell off, roast with a little bacon fat, and you will have a splendid cup of coffee.

2

Confederate Receipt Book:
A Compilation of Over One Hundred Receipts, Adapted to the Times

 Richmond: West & Johnston

 1863

 Rare Book and Special Collections Division

There came a point during the Civil War when Jefferson Davis, president of the Confederacy, suggested that rats were just as good as squirrels for a meal; it was an acknowledgment at the highest level that hostilities had taken a devastating toll on the South and its home front. Midway through the war, this small book provided acutely adjusted recipes for coping with severe shortages of food and household goods. If its subtitle delicately recognized a change in circumstances, the recipe names confirmed a turn for the worse: Apple Pie without Apples, Artificial Oysters, To Raise Bread without Yeast, Preserving Meat without Salt, Method of Curing Bad Butter, and Substitute for Coffee. At the time of the book's publication, in many Southern locales even the scant ingredients called for here were exorbitantly priced or impossible to find.

Recipe for Boston Brown Bread

From escaped slave to abolitionist, orator, author, and statesman, Frederick Douglass lived an extraordinary life that also included the ordinary—such as keeping a notebook of recipes. During the Civil War, Douglass recruited men for the Union cause at the African Meeting House in Boston, where he might well have obtained this recipe. The vague measurements include "as much water as is required."

As an enslaved child in Maryland, Douglass befriended a group of white boys who helped him learn to read. He later wrote in his autobiography that he used to carry bread with him, which "I used to bestow upon the hungry little urchins, who, in return, would give me that more valuable bread of knowledge."

Boston brown bread

6 oz yellow meal.
4 " rye "
1 " white flour
1 tea spoon salt } even full
1 " " soda }
½ pt. milk
2 large spoonsfull molasses
water enough to make a stiff dough.
Sift the 2 meals together then sift in flour & all
Add molasses, milk & soda dissolved & lastly
as much water as is desired required
Steam 4 hours in tight vessel.

Frederick Douglass (ca. 1817–1895)

undated

Frederick Douglass Papers, Manuscript Division

Recipe for Pork Cake

 Clara Barton
(1821–1912)

 1861

 Clara Barton Papers,
Manuscript Division

MEMORANDA.

Recipe for Pork cake —
13 oz pork chopped fine as possible - pour
1 pint of boiling water - two cups molasses
1 of sugar. - 1 lb of raisins cut once or twice -
2 tea spoonfuls saleratus, cloves - alspice + cinnamon
Frost if desired - add fruit or not
Bake considerable - (mix) very stiff —

"The Angel of the Battlefield" during the Civil War and later founder of the American Red Cross, Clara Barton was a self-taught nurse who tended to and cooked for wounded Union soldiers, coming within inches of being hit by shells that tore through her clothing on a couple of occasions. She used this pocket memorandum book to draft letters, keep grocery accounts, maintain a diary, and jot down this popular recipe. Pork cake, filled with common, inexpensive ingredients, was a staple in nineteenth-century American households, and variations of the recipe appeared regularly in newspapers and magazines. Like traditional mincemeat pies, pork cake combined meat and fruit, spices and sweets.

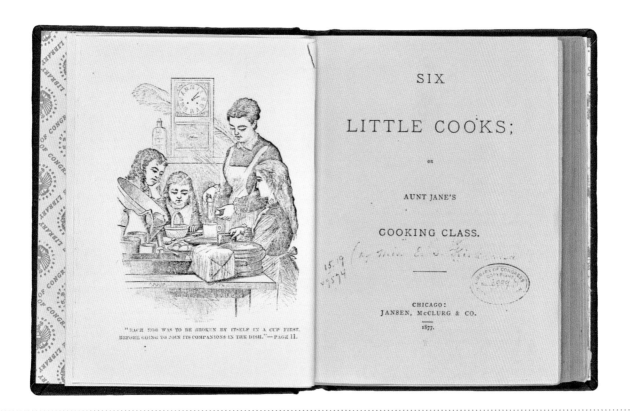

"EACH EGG WAS TO BE BROKEN BY ITSELF IN A CUP FIRST, BEFORE GOING TO JOIN ITS COMPANIONS IN THE DISH."—PAGE 11.

SIX

LITTLE COOKS;

OR

AUNT JANE'S

COOKING CLASS.

CHICAGO:
JANSEN, McCLURG & CO.
1877.

E. S. (Elizabeth Stansbury)
Kirkland (1828–1896)

Chicago: Jansen, McClurg

1877

General Collections

Six Little Cooks, or
Aunt Jane's Cooking Class

Cookbooks written expressly for children did not appear until the 1870s, with the publication of *Six Little Cooks*. This book is framed as a story about a woman, Aunt Jane, teaching her niece and her friends how to cook during a summer visit. The little cooks-in-training learn more than two hundred recipes, including one for a fudge-like concoction called "soft candy"—remarkable considering fudge did not become popular until the late 1880s.

What Mrs. Fisher Knows about Old Southern Cooking,

Soups, Pickles, Preserves, etc.

 Abby Fisher (1831–ca. 1910s)

 San Francisco: Women's Co-operative Printing Office

 1881

 Katherine Golden Bitting Collection on Gastronomy, Rare Book and Special Collections Division

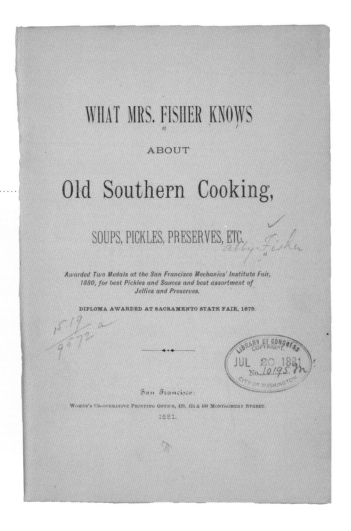

Born to a white plantation owner and an enslaved African-American woman in South Carolina, Abby Fisher (sometimes spelled Abbie) moved to California with her husband in 1877. The two of them operated a successful pickling business, and she won multiple prizes for her pickles, sauces, and jellies at state fairs. Encouraged by affluent San Francisco housekeepers and socialites, she dictated this cookbook, admitting in the preface that she was unable "to read or write myself." The 150 recipes reflect her thirty-five years of cooking experience, often imbuing "African aromas," per cookbook historian Toni Tipton-Martin. They include both Southern and other regional dishes, such as "ochra" gumbo and clam chowder, respectively. After the 1906 San Francisco earthquake, record of her book vanished, until one came up for auction in 1984. It is now credited as the earliest-known cookbook written by a formerly enslaved woman.

The Cosmopolitan Cook and Recipe Book

Dingens Brothers

Buffalo: E. H. Hutchinson

1882

General Collections

The proprietors of a Buffalo-based grocery compiled this guide to "provide the Public with a cheap but honest and practical Cook Book."

Having underwritten the publication with advertisements, the authors offered to send free copies to those unable to purchase one, especially house servants. Featuring recipes classified by ingredient and with detailed instructions for preparation, the *Cosmopolitan* anticipated the framework of contemporary cookbooks. A guide on measurements warns of variations in the sizes of household spoons, and an instructional essay from "The Widow Prudence" championed the inclusion of recipes using "all parts of the animal," including hearts, brains, trotters, kidneys, and heels.

1. *Groseilles à la Crême.* 2. *Cheese Fondu.* 3. *Trifle.* 4. *Ribbon Jelly.* 5. *Garibaldi Cream.* 6. *Tipsy Cake.* 7. *Ice Pudding.* 8. *Plovers Eggs and Aspic Jelly.* 9. *Strawberry Trifle.* 10. *Red Crystalised Oranges.* 11. *Beignets d' Orange.*

The New York Cook Book:
A Complete Manual of Cookery, in All Its Branches

Marie Martinelo

New York: J. Miller

1882

Katherine Golden Bitting Collection on Gastronomy, Rare Book and Special Collections Division

This vibrant chromolithograph highlights popular Gilded Age desserts like Garibaldi cream, ribbon jelly, ice pudding, strawberry trifle, and beignets d'orange. These desserts appeared as an addendum to the main text, adapted from recipes by Eliza Leslie, a popular cookbook writer earlier in the nineteenth century. Though the depicted delicacies are rarely served in twenty-first-century America, this would not surprise author Marie Martinelo, who wrote that "the fashions of the cuisine, like those of the dress, are subject to changes."

Community Cookbooks:
Fundraising with Food

STARTING IN THE SECOND HALF OF THE NINETEENTH CENTURY, COOKBOOK SALES BECAME A POPULAR WAY TO RAISE FUNDS FOR SCHOOLS, RELIGIOUS INSTITUTIONS, LIBRARIES, CHARITIES, AND OTHER LOCAL CAUSES. THESE COMMUNITY COOKBOOKS—ALSO CALLED CIVIC OR CHURCH COOKBOOKS—WERE ALMOST EXCLUSIVELY CREATED BY WOMEN IN A COLLECTIVE ENTERPRISE, WITH A VARIETY OF CONTRIBUTORS. THE BOOKS OFTEN INCLUDED LOCAL ADVERTISEMENTS, PROVIDING INSIGHT INTO COMMUNITY BUSINESS PRACTICES AND CULTURE. PERHAPS AS MANY AS 6,000 COMMUNITY COOKBOOKS WERE PUBLISHED BETWEEN THE CIVIL WAR AND THE GREAT DEPRESSION, THOUGH THEY CONTINUE TO BE PUBLISHED AND ARE ACTIVELY COLLECTED BY THE LIBRARY OF CONGRESS.

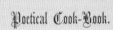

A Poetical Cook-book

Maria J. Moss, Philadelphia: C. Sherman, 1864. Katherine Golden Bitting Collection on Gastronomy, Rare Book and Special Collections Division.

Considered the first community cookbook, *A Poetical Cook-book* was sold to raise funds for the medical care of Union soldiers during the Civil War. Unlike most books in the genre, it had a single author, Maria J. Moss. Serving as an organizer of the Great Sanitary Fair in her native Philadelphia in 1864, Moss offered to sell this book of previously written recipes, dedicating it to "our suffering soldiers, the sick, wounded, and needy, who have so nobly fought our country's cause, to maintain the flag of our great Republic." She included amusing poems and couplets about food and cookery; her note to the reader is a five-page rhyming poem. The book was a success, inspiring other community groups to publish and sell their own cookbooks. As one visitor to the fair remarked, the cookbook "was all the more appreciated by the purchasers" who "felt that while they were gratifying their taste, they were also helping on a great work of charity."

Housekeeping in the Blue Grass

Edited by the Ladies of the Presbyterian Church, Paris, Kentucky. Cincinnati: G. E. Stevens, 1875. General Collections.

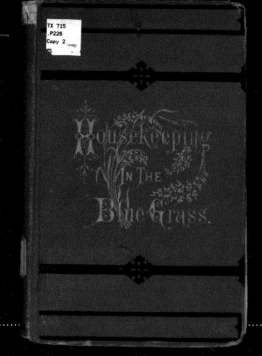

Community cookbooks often reflect local pride. This one sets the scene in its preface: "The Blue Grass region of Kentucky … is celebrated for the fertility of its soil, the beauty of its pastures, its flocks and blooded stock, and last, but not least, for the hospitality of its people and their table luxuries." Typical of the era, the recipes featured hyperlocal ingredients. For example, a recipe for pickling walnuts instructs the reader to "gather walnuts about the 10th of June." The First Presbyterian Church of Paris has continued its cookbook tradition into the twenty-first century, releasing *Feeding the Flock* in 2009.

Gulf City Cook Book

Compiled by the Ladies of St. Francis Street Methodist Episcopal Church, Mobile, Alabama. Dayton, Ohio: United Brethren Publishing House, 1878. General Collections.

This cookbook shows how French, African, and indigenous cultures influenced the cuisine of the Mississippi Gulf Coast. Recipes include this one for a very early version of jambalaya; instructions for making a

JAM BOLAYA.

Have the lard hot, put in flour, cook to a light brown, with a medium-sized onion. Take the giblets, neck, small part of the wings and feet of your chicken, and put in the lard; add half a tea-cup of prepared tomatoes, two dozen oysters, with their liquor, pepper and salt to taste; put in nearly a pint of rice, one table-spoonful of butter; stir frequently when nearly done; set back on the stove and let steam.

barbeque pit; a recipe for gumbo powder from sassafras leaves; and detailed directions on how to slaughter a turtle for soup. A remedy for sick turkeys calls for feeding the bird tar and brandy or whiskey.

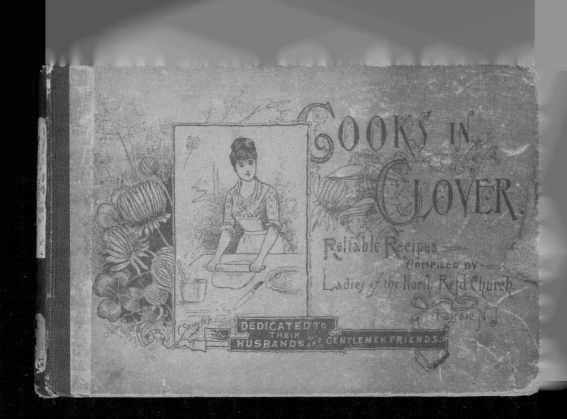

Cooks in Clover: Reliable Recipes

Compiled by the Ladies of the North Reformed Church. Passaic, NJ: The Church; Thurston & Barker, 1889. General Collections.

This beautiful cover announces that the compilers have dedicated the book "to their husbands and gentlemen friends." The first section contains advertising for local businesses before providing recipes organized in traditional cookbook groupings. Culinary and medicinal recipes for "the Sick Room" include one for toast water (the liquid remaining when stale bread is boiled in hot water). A concluding section of hints recommends

Barman and Showman

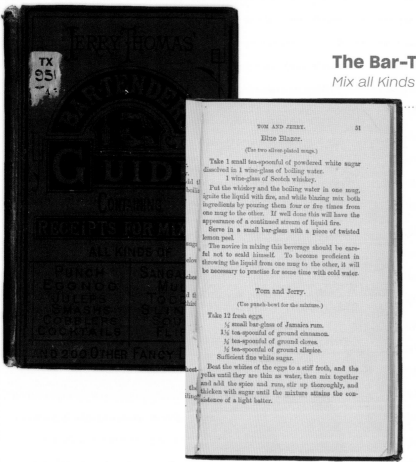

The Bar-Tender's Guide, *or How to Mix all Kinds of Plain and Fancy Drinks*

Jerry Thomas (1830–1885)

New York: Dick & Fitzgerald

1887

General Collections

Perhaps no one person put their mark on American cocktails more than Jerry Thomas, who revolutionized mixology with flashy showmanship behind the bar. Born in upstate New York, he became a sailor and eventually ended up in California during the Gold Rush, where he worked as a gold prospector and bartender and managed a minstrel show troupe, sharpening his theatrical talents. Returning east, he opened his first New York City bar in 1851 in the basement of P. T. Barnum's American Museum. Over the next thirty-five years, he developed a larger-than-life persona and became America's first celebrity bartender. Touring the

The Bon Vivant's Companion, or How to Mix Drinks, *edited and with an introduction by Herbert Asbury*

 Jerry Thomas (1830–1885)

 New York: A. A. Knopf

 1928

 General Collections

country and opening new bars in San Francisco and New York, he wore diamonds, loved fancy gloves and watches, and perched white rats on his shoulders as he mixed drinks. He displayed caricatures of celebrities by renowned cartoonist Thomas Nast in his New York bar, which attracted patrons who came expressly to view them.

Prior bartenders had either kept recipes to themselves as trade secrets or passed them down orally to apprentices. But Thomas made history by publishing the first drink recipe book in 1862, the landmark *How to Mix Drinks*, in which he memorialized his recipes for cocktails, punches, cobblers, and other types of beverages. Later editions, including the posthumous 1887 edition (opposite), expanded the cocktail list to include the first written recipe for a Tom Collins and Thomas's famous Blue Blazer. Created at the El Dorado saloon in San Francisco, this fiery concoction involves setting whiskey on fire and pouring it between two silver-plated mugs as seen above in the frontispiece to the 1928 edition. Thomas also invented the Tom and Jerry recipe (opposite).

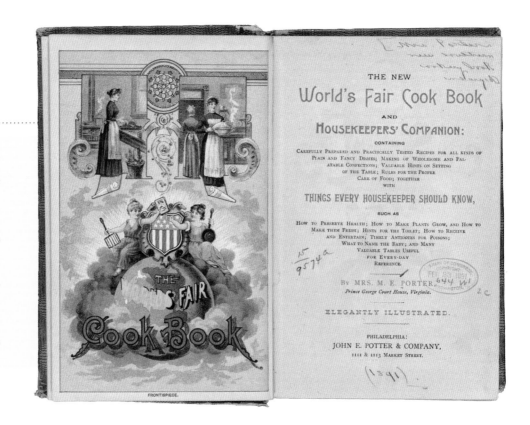

M. E. Porter

Philadelphia:
J. E. Potter

1891

General
Collections

The New World's Fair Cook Book and Housekeepers' Companion:
Things Every Housekeeper Should Know

This generically titled unofficial tie-in to the 1893 World's Columbian Exposition (also known as the Chicago World's Fair) was available even to those who were not among the fair's 27 million visitors. Mrs. M. E. Porter enlarged, updated, and repackaged her earlier work, *Mrs. Porter's New Southern Cookery Book* (1871), in anticipation of the Windy City's landmark event. Given the somewhat vague language that frequently appeared in cookbook instructions at the time, her publisher assured readers that the recipes were "written in plain English, concisely yet clearly, so that none can mistake their meaning." As a further example of quality control, "competent housewives and successful cooks" had tested each entry. With nearly 800 recipes (more than half are for sweets and desserts), the hefty, 485-page hardcover tome was best purchased when leaving the fairgrounds.

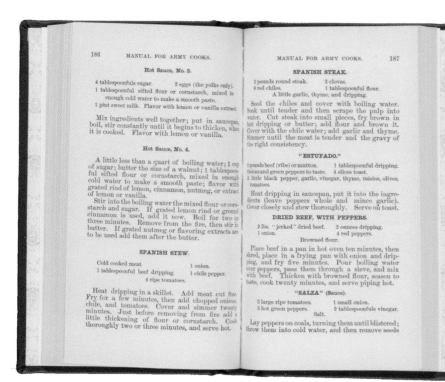

Manual for Army Cooks

US War Department, Subsistence Department

Washington, DC: Government Printing Office

1896

General Collections

This classic US military cookbook was in use during the Spanish-American War (1898), with recipes for meals in garrison and in the field. Hot sauce has long been a regular condiment for army meals, in part to obscure other aspects of traditional army food, and four recipes for it are included here. But this government volume was a culinary revelation, providing basic, healthy menus and branching out to feature a number of Spanish and Mexican dishes, such as *frijoles con queso*, stuffed green chiles, and Spanish rice. A recipe for "salza" noted that it should "be served with soup or meat as a relish." Even the *Boston Cooking School Magazine*, in 1901, reprinted the army's recipe for tamales. Reviewing the book shortly after its release, food critic E. F. Hannah wrote, "The tables of contents alone of the manual are almost enough to rouse one's patriotism to the enlisting point."

The Century Cook Book and Home Physician

Jennie Adrienné Hansey (1843–1918) and Dr. N. T. Oliver (1859–1940)

Chicago: Laird & Lee

1897

General Collections

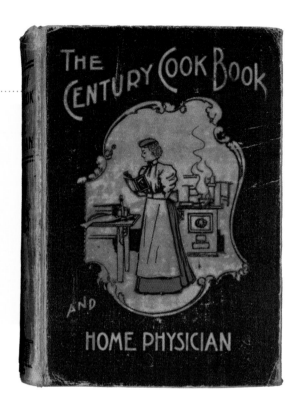

Though written before the dawn of the twentieth century, *The Century Cook Book and Home Physician* contained an overall structure and individual recipes, such as egg salad, beef stew, and ginger snaps, familiar to readers of contemporary cookbooks. Yet the book is not without its late nineteenth-century quirks. For example, the section on vegetables is unusually expansive, including traditional recipes like stewed carrots and boiled cauliflower alongside recipes for carb-heavy items such as mashed potatoes, macaroni and cheese, and something called Corn in the Ear. A section on "Artistic Cookery" includes instructions and illustrations for such delicacies as Filets of Snipes in Cases and Lambs' Brains a L'Italienne. The second half of the book focuses on housekeeping and health, with instructions for cleaning corsets, removing foreign bodies from the nose, and preparing the perfect linseed meal poultice. The advice for alleviating hysteria—an affliction apparently limited to women—starts with loosening the dress and ends with a "dash of cold water upon the face."

Jennie Adrienné Hansey also wrote under the pseudonym of Ella M. Blackstone. Dr. N. T. Oliver was a pen name for Edward Oliver Tilburn, also known as "Nevada Ned." This colorful author—whose claim to be a graduate of Yale was one of many falsehoods advanced in a long life—was an actor, a purveyor of patent medicine, a preacher, and a serial swindler.

Advertisement for Club Cocktails

G. F. Heublein & Bro.

The Illustrated American 24, no. 20

November 18, 1898

General Collections

Heublien began as a restaurant in 1862, but by the end of the nineteenth century, it changed its focus to selling canned cocktails such as Martinis, Manhattans, and York cocktails (equal parts scotch and dry vermouth, three dashes of orange bitters, and a lemon twist). Though bottled cocktails date to the mid-nineteenth century, Heublein first started its Club Cocktails—named after the club cars of Pullman trains—in 1892 and they became the industry standard.

One reason canned cocktails were so popular at this time is that the art of mixing drinks was usually reserved to bartenders like Jerry Thomas—thus the attraction of having "a better cocktail at home than is served over any bar in the world." Though canned cocktails' popularity waxed and waned in the second half of the twentieth century, they've had a resurgence: from 2009 to 2019, the "ready to drink" category grew by 214 percent, according to one estimate. And 2020 saw a 162 percent increase, fueled in part by the COVID-19 pandemic that shut down many bars and restaurants, leading to more at-home drinking.

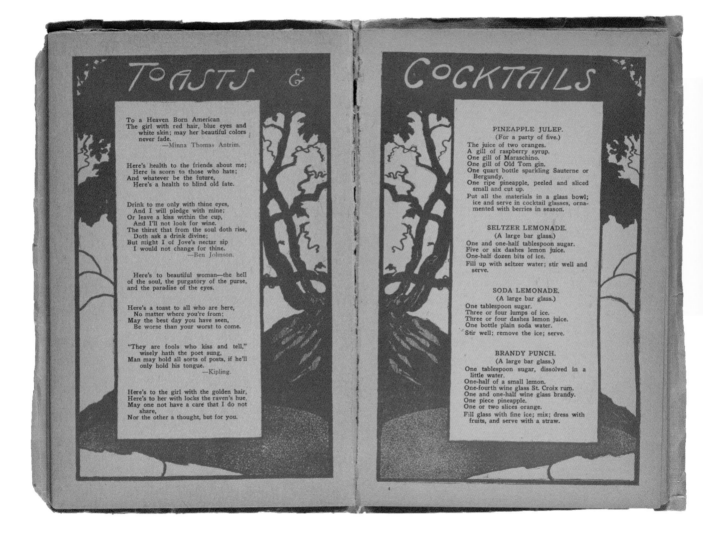

TOASTS & COCKTAILS

TOASTS

To a Heaven Born American
The girl with red hair, blue eyes and
white skin; may her beautiful colors
never fade.
—Minna Thomas Antrim.

Here's health to the friends about me;
Here is scorn to those who hate;
And whatever be the future,
Here's a health to blind old fate.

Drink to me only with thine eyes,
And I will pledge with mine;
Or leave a kiss within the cup,
And I'll not look for wine.
The thirst that from the soul doth rise,
Doth ask a drink divine;
But might I of Jove's nectar sip
I would not change for thine.
—Ben Johnson.

Here's to beautiful woman—the hell
of the soul, the purgatory of the purse,
and the paradise of the eyes.

Here's a toast to all who are here,
No matter where you're from;
May the best day you have seen,
Be worse than your worst to come.

"They are fools who kiss and tell,"
wisely hath the poet sung,
Man may hold all sorts of posts, if he'll
only hold his tongue.
—Kipling.

Here's to the girl with the golden hair,
Here's to her with locks the raven's hue,
May one not have a care that I do not
share,
Nor the other a thought, but for you.

COCKTAILS

PINEAPPLE JULEP.
(For a party of five.)
The juice of two oranges.
A gill of raspberry syrup.
One gill of Maraschino.
One gill of Old Tom gin.
One quart bottle sparkling Sauterne or
Bergundy.
One ripe pineapple, peeled and sliced
small and cut up.
Put all the materials in a glass bowl;
ice and serve in cocktail glasses, orna-
mented with berries in season.

SELTZER LEMONADE.
(A large bar glass.)
One and one-half tablespoon sugar.
Five or six dashes lemon juice.
One-half dozen bits of ice.
Fill up with seltzer water; stir well and
serve.

SODA LEMONADE.
(A large bar glass.)
One tablespoon sugar.
Three or four lumps of ice.
Three or four dashes lemon juice.
One bottle plain soda water.
Stir well; remove the ice; serve.

BRANDY PUNCH.
(A large bar glass.)
One tablespoon sugar, dissolved in a
little water.
One-half of a small lemon.
One-fourth wine glass St. Croix rum.
One and one-half wine glass brandy.
One piece pineapple.
One or two slices orange.
Fill glass with fine ice; mix; dress with
fruits, and serve with a straw.

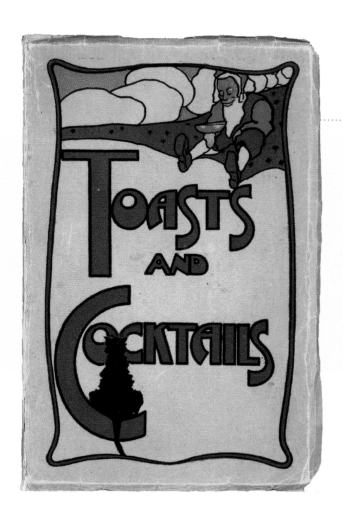

Toasts and Cocktails

 Harry A. Rodgers

 St. Louis: Shallcross Printing & Stationery

 1905

 Katherine Golden Bitting Collection on Gastronomy, Rare Book and Special Collections Division

Tinted in Christmas colors of green and red, the cover of this 1905 treasure features a besotted-looking Santa gripping a large glass and dozing, while a cat perched on the "C" of "Cocktails" looks on. Each left-hand page features a collection of toasts. Some, like Ben Johnson's

"Drink to me only with thine eyes," are lyrical. Others are unsigned and cutting: "A woman's tongue is only three inches long, but it can kill a man six feet high." The cocktail recipes range from a lively, alcohol-free seltzer lemonade to an intoxicating Brandy Champerelle that combines four liqueurs and three drops of bitters into an ice-free glass over an inverted spoon.

Votes and Victuals

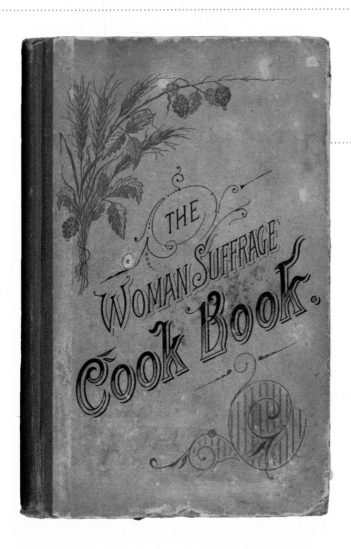

The Woman Suffrage Cook Book

 Hattie A. Burr, ed.

 Boston: C. H. Simonds Printers

 1886

Rare Book and Special Collections Division

When it came to money-raising cookbook projects, women's suffrage was a natural cause, and at least six such works were published between 1886 and 1920, including the two pictured here. More than 160 women from around the country contributed to Hattie A. Burr's version, which also included a section of "eminent opinions on woman suffrage." The book's goal was to show that women who wished to vote would still "cherish a feminine interest in culinary matters," as one newspaper report put it.

The Suffrage Cook Book

 Mrs. L. O. Kleber, ed.

 Pittsburgh: Equal Franchise
Federation of Western Pennsylvania

 1915

 General Collections

Mrs. Kleber's book featured Uncle Sam on the cover calmly balancing a scale of the sexes, as well as an image of the sun with rays depicting the states that already granted women full or partial voting rights. The book's tagline, "The Best Cooks are Suffragists," sought to link women's domestic skills with their ability to solve the nation's problems through the ballot box. For example, one tongue-in-cheek recipe for Pie for a Suffragist's Doubting Husband listed ills like war, child labor, and impure food as items that "the milk of human kindness" could make into a tasty pie with a crust mixed by a woman's "tact and velvet gloves."

Lehr-bukh vi azoy tsu kokhen un baken

[Textbook on How to Cook and Bake]

Hinde Amchanitzki
(ca. 1823–1910)

New York: n.p.

1901

African & Middle
Eastern Division

The first Yiddish cookbook published in America—in fact, one of the first in the world—includes traditional Jewish recipes alongside instructions for foods that may have been exotic to newly arriving immigrants, such as English pot roast, hamburger steak, oatmeal, and banana pie. Pictured on the cover, Hinde Amchanitzki was born in Russia and immigrated to America in 1895. After working in kitchens of private homes and restaurants for forty-five years, she decided to share her recipes with other immigrants by writing them down in this cookbook. Like contemporaneous American cookbooks written in English, *Lehr-bukh vi azoy tsu kokhen un baken* included medicinal recipes.

The Boston Cooking School, founded in 1879, taught women how to cook using a scientific-based curriculum that incorporated precise measurements, nutrition, and diet. Fannie Farmer, a student and later principal of the school, published *The Boston Cooking-School Cook Book* in 1896 and it quickly became one of the best-selling cookbooks in America. Farmer believed the book's use of standardized measurements and "condensed scientific knowledge" would "lead to deeper thought and broader study of what to eat." The book was highly successful, selling over seven million copies and influencing generations of cooks to use a more scientific approach in the kitchen.

Capitalizing on the fame of *The Boston Cooking-School Cook Book*, Farmer developed seven other cookbooks, including *A New Book of Cookery*, originally published in 1912. Unlike the original *Boston* cookbook, which only had black and white images, her new book featured eight vibrant color images, including this one of a frosted ham. *A New Book of Cookery* contains 860 recipes, eighteen of which are just for frosting. The frosted ham recipe calls for "ornamental frosting," made of confectioner's sugar, eggs, and cream of tartar.

A New Book of Cookery

 Fannie Merritt Farmer (1857–1915)

 Boston: Little, Brown

 1915 reprint

 General Collections

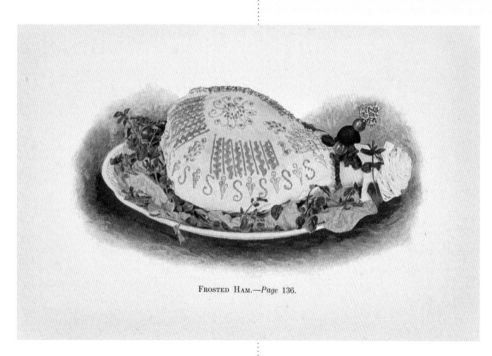

FROSTED HAM.—*Page* 136.

"Here's looking at you!"

 Lou Mayer

 Cover illustration, photomechanical print

 September 12, 1914

 Prints and Photographs Division

Puck was America's first major humor magazine, and it published satirical covers, cartoons, and articles from 1871 to 1918. Cocktail glasses like the one shown here—related but different from their slightly larger, less round cousin, the martini glass—date to the late nineteenth century. Used for cocktails served "straight up," i.e., without ice, the long stem prevents the drinker's hand from accidentally warming up the libation, while the large bowl enhances aromatic elements of the cocktail.

The Ideal Bartender

 Tom Bullock (1873–1964)

 St. Louis: Buxton & Skinner

 1917

 General Collections

The Ideal Bartender was the first cocktail book published by an African-American author, Tom Bullock, seen here in the book's frontispiece. Bullock worked as a bartender at the St. Louis Country Club and published this book of 173 recipes during World War I, just before the onset of Prohibition. His Mint Julep was so appealing that when a supposedly sober Theodore Roosevelt claimed to have imbibed just a sip or two, a newspaper retorted that it was impossible to taste one of Bullock's drinks without finishing it. One patron of the club who also enjoyed Bullock's drinks was George Herbert Walker, the grandfather and great-grandfather of the two Bush presidents. Walker wrote the introduction to *The Ideal Bartender*.

Dehydrated food luncheon at Senate

In 1942, the US Senate restaurant kitchen served a meal of dehydrated foods to show lawmakers what military personnel were eating abroad.

 George Danor (1913–1978)

 Nitrate negative

 December 1942

 Farm Security Administration/Office of War Information Collection, Prints and Photographs Division

CHAPTER 3

Palatable Dishes with Simple Means"

COOKING IN DESPERATE TIMES

Cookbooks in the first half of the twentieth century mirrored the rise of middle-class consumerism in America and the transition to standardized measurements and cooking techniques. These books frequently targeted homemakers rather than professional household cooks. Though the Great Depression led to 25 percent unemployment—one result of which was New York City charitable groups doling out 85,000 meals a day—cookbooks continued to sell during the 1930s. Some focused on economizing in the kitchen, but most instructions featured ingredients that could only be purchased with pre-Crash budgets.

World War II also had a dramatic impact on American cookery. Wartime rations led to limits on sugar, coffee, meats and fish, dairy products, and certain cooking fats. As President Franklin D. Roosevelt said in a 1942 fireside chat, "There is one front and one battle where everyone in the United States—every man, woman, and child—is in action, and will be privileged to remain in action throughout this war. That front is right here at home, in our daily lives, and in our daily tasks." Meanwhile, military personnel overseas had to rely on "C-Rations," tin cans filled with items such as corned beef, bacon, or hardtack biscuits. For prisoners of war, the food offerings were even bleaker, ironically leading many to record recipes featuring foods they could only dream of.

This period also saw the onset and eventual repeal of Prohibition (1920–1933), which made illegal the manufacture, sale, and transportation of intoxicating beverages. Though public consumption of alcohol declined during the thirteen-plus years of Prohibition, drinking continued privately, irrevocably changing American cocktail culture. Prior to Prohibition, saloons and barrooms run by the likes of Jerry Thomas had usually been the purview of men. Now speakeasies catered equally to men and women, and flappers often were their biggest patrons.

Unknown photographer

Photographic print

ca. 1921

Prints and Photographs Division

New York City Deputy Police Commissioner John A. Leach watching agents pour liquor into sewer

Prohibition changed what, where, and with whom Americans drank. As evidenced by this photo, the police were tasked with destroying liquor, which led to bootleggers clandestinely producing their own bathtub gin and moonshine. Fueled by this illegal alcohol, drinks with liquor increased from about 33 percent of all alcoholic beverages prior to 1920 to 75 percent by 1930. Famous cocktails like the Sidecar, Bee's Knees, and the Mary Pickford date to this period. Still, alcohol remained in short supply, and a night out at a speakeasy got very expensive. Much cocktail drinking during this period was done at home, via whatever alcohol and mixers Americans could get their hands on.

Macaroni with Italian Sauce

100 quarts—700 servings

24 pounds macaroni	9½ ounces butterine
18 gallon cans tomato	4 pounds salt
¼ ounce soda	1½ ounces pepper
1 pound 12 ounces salt pork	2 pounds 4 ounces sugar
9 quarts flour	1 pound onions
9 quarts water	4 pounds American cheese

Break macaroni into small pieces, cook until soft; blanch. Put into pans one-third full. Strain tomato into container, add soda. Try out salt pork and use fat to bind thickening. Add thickening to strained tomatoes. Cook until it comes to boiling point. Remove from fire, add butterine, salt, pepper, sugar, and chopped onion. Add cheese cut into small pieces. Cook mixture until smooth. Pour over macaroni in pans, cover with buttered crumbs and brown in oven.

SCHOOL LUNCHEONS,
WOMAN'S EDUCATIONAL AND INDUSTRIAL UNION

Recipes for Institutions

🍳 Chicago Dietetic Association

🗄 New York: Macmillan

⏱ 1922

📖 General Collections

Any recipe that calls for four pounds of cheese and twenty-four pounds of noodles can't be all bad—the only downside might be having to share that dish with 699 others. More than seventy dietitians contributed recipes to this pioneering work primarily for use in hospital and school cafeterias, providing quality in a field where quantity naturally comes in bulk, such as a three-quart No. 10 can of tomatoes. (The recipe for Southern Bisque calls for fifteen such cans.) A section on special diets includes recipes for diabetics, anemics, and typhoid fever patients, the latter being not uncommon at the time. Even a volunteer committee member taking on large-scale social gatherings could make good use of the book. As the *New-York Tribune* noted, "salad dressings in gallon lots; cookies and sandwiches by the hundred; all these recipes worked out in large proportions would make any woman a pillar of the church."

Cocktail Time *from the musical revue* Mayfair and Montmartre

 Cole Porter (1891–1964)

 London and New York: Chappell & Co. Ltd.

 1922

 Music Division

Cole Porter was one of the most popular composers from the 1920s through the 1940s, known for musicals such as *Anything Goes* and *Kiss Me Kate*. He contributed three songs to the 1922 musical revue *Mayfair and Montmartre*, based on a book by Ralph Nevill, which premiered at London's New Oxford Theatre. The musical also included songs by well-known composers such as Irving Berlin and George Gershwin. While the show ran for seventy-seven performances, critics gave it mixed reviews, though

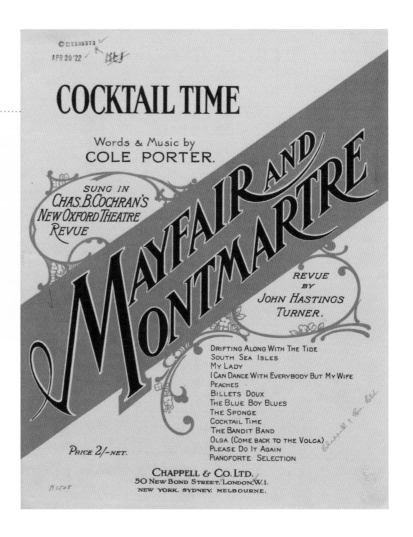

mostly for the sketches and not the music. With no Prohibition in Great Britain, the lyrics of "Cocktail Time" could directly reference drinking without the need for innuendo, such as the opening bit: "I must be on my way/I haven't time to stay/The reason is because/It's Cocktail Time."

800 Proved Pecan Recipes:
Their Place in the Menu by 5,083 Housewives

Nothing says group effort like a book with more than five thousand authors. These pecan recipes, which cover "every phase of every meal, for all seasons of the year," were selected from some 21,000 that were tested by "skilled dietitians" at the Keystone Pecan Research Laboratory in Manheim, Pennsylvania. This specialty cookbook showcased "Nature's finest, most concentrated food product . . . fitted to the crying need for a low protein diet" now that "telephone, automobiles and labor-saving devices" meant that the public no longer needed "to follow the heavy protein diet of our forefathers . . . a certain method of overtaxing one's kidneys and leading to disastrous results." The recipe for the pecan sandwich loaf shown here calls for bread coated in creamed cheese with hard-cooked egg, lettuce, chopped olive, and raisin fillings. The decorative exterior pecan design is deliberately left up to one's own artistic vision and skill.

 Keystone Pecan Company

 Manheim, PA: Keystone Pecan Research Laboratory

 1925

 Rare Book and Special Collections Division

Aunt Sammy's Radio Recipes

 Bureau of Home Economics,
United States Department of Agriculture

 Washington, DC: Government Printing Office

 1927

 General Collections

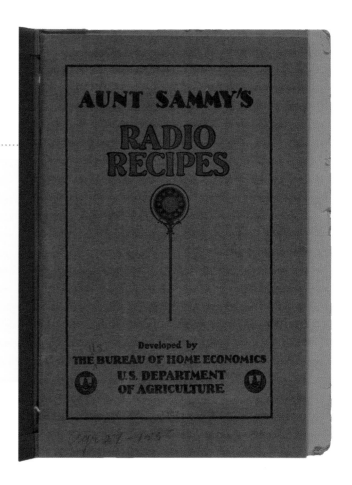

One of the earliest celebrity cooks to hit the airwaves was Aunt Sammy—generally regarded as the wife of Uncle Sam—who debuted on the weekday *Housekeeper's Chat* radio show in 1926. The US Bureau of Home Economics cooked up the friendly character to share improved and efficient household practices with the public, and Aunt Sammy was actually a team effort: Ruth Van Deman oversaw the menus and recipes that Aunt Sammy recommended, Fanny Walker Yeatman tested them, and Josephine Hemphill penned the show's lively scripts. "This is no caviar and truffle service for jazz-jaded appetites," Van Deman told the Associated Press. "We are striving to serve that great substantial class of women who are homemakers. We aim to make the menus simple, well balanced, delicious and also adaptable to the food supplies in all parts of the country." Eventually, the program aired on nearly 200 radio stations, but there was no single Aunt Sammy, as each station used its own performers to act out the show. In 1927, the bureau issued a half-million free *Radio Recipes* booklets, which listeners snapped up almost immediately. The show continued to air until 1944.

The Up-to-Date Sandwich Book: *555*
Ways to Make a Sandwich

Eva Greene Fuller

Chicago: A. C. McClurg

1927

General Collections

BANANA SANDWICH

Mash ripe bananas; add a dash of lemon juice; sweeten to taste. Place between thin slices of buttered white bread cut oblong.

BANANA SANDWICH NO. 2

On thin slices of lightly buttered white bread spread mayonnaise dressing then add thin slices of bananas; cover with another slice of bread. Serve on a lettuce leaf.

BANANA AND CHERRY SANDWICH

Mash three bananas fine, add one-half cup of chopped maraschino cherries, a tablespoonful of powdered sugar, moisten with a little thick cream, mix, and place between thin slices of lightly buttered white bread. Garnish with a cherry.

146

Just when sandwich aficionados thought that Eva Greene Fuller could not top her first popular sandwich compilation from 1909, which featured 400 recipes, she added 155 more to this expanded volume. (The timing of this second edition was inadvertently apt; the following year machine-sliced bread first went on the market.) From the routine chopped peanut and jelly on toast to the decadent caviar-lobster combo, Fuller maintained that the one constant "in the preparation of good sandwiches is to have perfect bread in suitable condition." One reviewer marveled that "if there is any way to make a sandwich, or any material to make it from that Miss Fuller has failed to discover, it can be left for arctic explorers and others who subsist on queer foods."

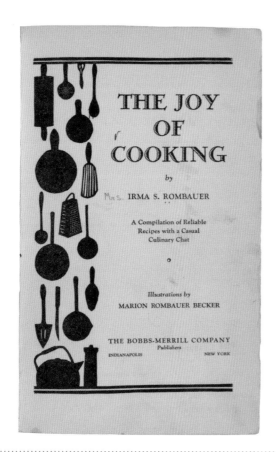

The Joy of Cooking:
A Compilation of Reliable Recipes,
with a Casual Culinary Chat

No person left a bigger mark on American cookbooks than Irma Rombauer, whose *Joy of Cooking* influenced the genre for decades. The origins of this story were anything but joyous: after her husband committed suicide following the stock market crash of 1929, Rombauer used her life savings to write and publish the book. She enlisted friends and relatives to test 500 recipes for what she called in the preface "palatable dishes with simple means." Her daughter Marion illustrated and designed the book, and she worked with local printer A. C. Slayton to print 3,000 copies.

The book was an instant success, in part thanks to its novel concept. Previously, most cookbooks gave recipes in paragraphs, with vague directions about how to put them together. Rombauer instead included personal anecdotes, what the subtitle described as "a casual culinary chat," and precise, separately listed ingredients in an easy-to-read format with detailed directions.

Soon Bobbs-Merill took over publication, though Rombauer and eventually her children remained involved. The book has since gone through nine editions, sold more than 20 million copies, and changed the way Americans cook. In 1998, a facsimile of the original 1931 edition was released, including Marion's cover illustration of St. Martha of Bethany, the patron saint of cooking, slaying the dragon of kitchen drudgery. In 2006, Scribner published a seventy-fifth anniversary edition with the famous red "joy" cover; National Braille Press later used that version to produce a thirty-volume edition for visually impaired cooks. And in 2012, The Library of Congress added *The Joy of Cooking* to its list of Books that Shaped America; the only other cookbook to make the list was Amelia Simmons's *American Cookery*.

 Irma S. Rombauer (1877–1962); illustrations by Marion Rombauer Becker (1903–1976)

 Indianapolis: Bobbs-Merrill, first trade edition

 1936

 General Collections

Irma S. Rombauer, Marion Rombauer Becker, and Ethan Becker (b. 1945), **The Joy of Cooking, 75th anniversary edition**, New York: Scribner, 2006, General Collections.

Irma S. Rombauer, **The Joy of Cooking, facsimile of original 1931 edition**, New York: Scribner, 1998, General Collections.

Irma S. Rombauer, Marion Rombauer Becker, and Ethan Becker, **The Joy of Cooking, braille version of 2006 print edition**, Boston: National Braille Press, 2010. National Library Service for the Blind and Print Disabled, Library of Congress. Photo by Shawn Miller.

Mexican Cookbook

Erna Fergusson (1888–1964); Woodcuts by Valentín Vidaurreta (1902–1955)

Santa Fe, NM: Rydal Press

1934

General Collections

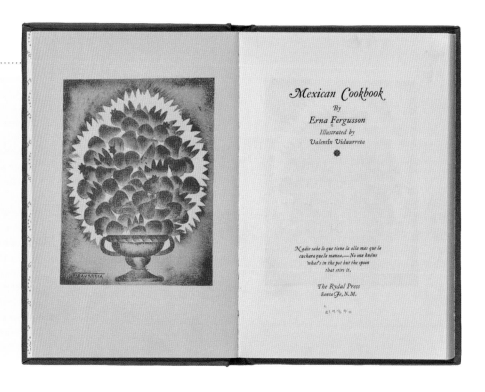

Reporter, adventure travel guide, and New Mexico's first lady of letters, Albuquerque native Erna Fergusson is remembered in culinary lore for her compact introduction to Mexican cookery, among the first to reach the American public at large. "The menus are based on meals as served at a gentleman's table before the general adoption of American ways," she wrote. "Then eating was a serious matter, interfered with only by famine, war, or Lent." Dolores "Lola" Chávez de Armijo, the New Mexico state librarian, supplied most of the recipes. Notably, Fergusson corrected the Anglo mistranslation of *frijoles refritos* as "refried beans"; in Spanish, the term instead means "fried beans" or "well-fried beans," but restaurant menus and canned food labels continue to say otherwise, and the misnomer remains in use.

Irvin S. Cobb's Own Recipe Book:

Containing Authoritative Directions for Making 71 Famous Drinks, Together with a Rollicking Dissertation of the Joys of King Bourbon and its Brother Rye

Irvin S. Cobb was a humorist, writer, editor, and native of Kentucky, a state well known for its bourbon. After the repeal of Prohibition in 1933, Frankfort Distilleries hired him to write a cocktail book, intended to reintroduce the public to the art of drink making. In addition to a section on drink recipes, he included a corporate history of Frankfort Distilleries, an overview of bourbon and rye, and waxed rhapsodic about juleps, "the queen mother of all the infusions."

This edition, published two years after the original 1934 version, includes the bookplate of the Katherine Golden Bitting Collection on Gastronomy. Bitting (1868–1937), a food chemist for the Department of Agriculture, amassed a personal collection of materials about growing, preparing, cooking, preserving, and eating food. After Bitting died, her husband presented the 4,346-volume collection to the Library of Congress.

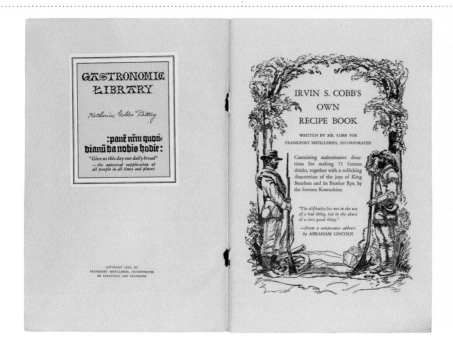

 Irvin S. Cobb
(1876–1944)

 Louisville: Frankfort Distilleries, second edition

 1936

 Katherine Golden Bitting Collection on Gastronomy, Rare Book and Special Collections Division

Draft rum label

 Franklin D. Roosevelt (1882–1945)

 ca. 1934–1937

Harold L. Ickes Papers,
Manuscript Division

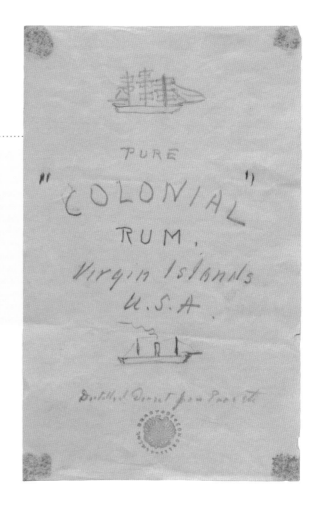

Franklin D. Roosevelt loved Martinis, and the cocktail industry certainly loved him after he pushed for the repeal of Prohibition during his first year in the White House. Upon issuing Presidential Proclamation 2065, confirming that the Twenty-first Amendment repealing Prohibition had passed, he reportedly mixed the nation's first legal Martini in fourteen years. And throughout his presidency, he often broke out a cocktail shaker during what he called "Children's Hour," an informal gathering with his top advisors.

After Prohibition ended, the US Government got into the alcohol business. FDR and his advisors chose the US Virgin Islands as a place to manufacture rum. The Public Works Administration invested $1 million in the project, and FDR got personally involved, creating this label to advocate for his suggested name of "Colonial Rum." Instead, the rum was named "Government House." Writer David Embury said of it: "I have never yet tasted a good Virgin Islands rum, but Old St. Croix and Cruzan are probably the best I have tried and Government House the worst."

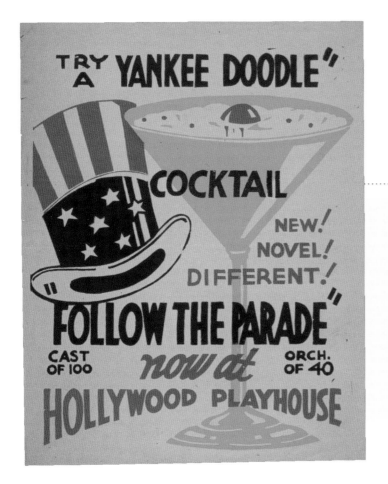

Try a Yankee Doodle Cocktail - New! Novel! Different! - "Follow the Parade" Now at Hollywood Playhouse

Federal Theatre Project

California: Federal Art Project, silkscreen color print

1936

Prints and Photographs Division

A tertiary dictionary definition of "cocktail" notes that it can be "any diverse mixture of elements, especially one with a powerful effect," which explains the image used in advertising for *Follow the Parade*. Billed as "A Satirical, Topical, Musical Revue in Two Parts," the show included segments set in Russia, Hawaii, a magic toy shop, a Harlem night club, a prison cell, and the home of the famous Dionne Quintuplets. A scene called the "Crazy House Suite" featured such numbers as "The Absent Minded Princess" and "March of the Lunatic Puppets." *Follow the Parade* was the first musical from the Federal Theatre Project, a New Deal initiative to employ entertainers, and it enjoyed a successful run in Southern California. The indefatigable Eda Edson, a former Broadway vaudevillian, was credited with the show's conception, direction, staging, and choreography; she did not have a role on stage as she also served as conductor of the orchestra.

Henrietta Nesbitt and the FDR White House

THE FOOD SERVED IN THE WHITE HOUSE CARRIES SYMBOLIC MEANING, WHETHER REPRESENTING THE NATION AT STATE FUNCTIONS OR PROMOTING HEALTHY EATING. PERHAPS NO PRESIDENTIAL ADMINISTRATION BETTER EXEMPLIFIED THIS FACT THAN THAT OF FRANKLIN D. ROOSEVELT, WHO LIVED IN THE WHITE HOUSE LONGER THAN ANY OTHER OCCUPANT.

FROZEN PINEAPPLE CHEESE SALAD   SALAD

1 t. gelatin
2 packages (6 oz.) cream cheese
2 T. cold water
3 T. cooked salad dressing
¼ t. salt
⅛ t. paparika
1 C crushed pineapple
½ c. cream, whipped

Method: Soak gelatin in cold water five minutes and dissolve over boiling water. Mash cheese and add salad dressing, salt, pepper and dissolved gelatin. Add pineapple, drained of its juice, and fold in whipped cream. Add one half cup chopped nuts. Turn into freezing trays. Serve in nest of lettuce and garnish with cherries.

Frozen Pineapple Cheese Salad

Undated. Henrietta Nesbitt Papers, Manuscript Division.

When the Roosevelts moved into the White House, the country was suffering from the Great Depression. Eleanor Roosevelt wanted economical meals, such as cracker pie, served in the White House to set an example for the nation, but the result was sometimes lackluster. Ernest Hemingway remarked after visiting in 1937, "We had a rainwater soup followed by rubber squab, a nice wilted salad and a cake some admirer had sent in. An enthusiastic but unskilled admirer." President Roosevelt occasionally complained about the food, as evidenced in the letter shown opposite. Henrietta Nesbitt, the head housekeeper, tried to heed his wishes, but Eleanor Roosevelt often overruled his requests. Nonetheless, he did enjoy certain recipes such as pig hocks, or pig knuckles.

Though Nesbitt did not personally do the cooking, she oversaw the cooks, making sure each dish was to her satisfaction. She later wrote two books about her time serving as the Roosevelt's housekeeper: *White House Diary* (1948) and *Presidential Cookbook: Feeding the Roosevelts and Their Guests* (1951), the latter of which contained dozens of recipes from her time as the Roosevelts' housekeeper. The Library of Congress acquired her papers in 1959.

Cracker Pie recipe

Undated. Henrietta Nesbitt Papers, Manuscript Division.

Cracker Pie

12 Trenton crackers rolled as fine as flour with the rolling pin (9 crackers)

3/4 lb. sugar (8 ozs)

3 ozs. butter (2 ozs)

4 eggs (3 eggs) beaten separately, add whites last

1 Pint Milk (2 2/3) gills.

Rind 1 lemon grated, juice

2 lemons (rind of 2/3 of a lemon + juice of about 1 1/3 —)

This recipe as given is said to make 3 pies — I use about

About 2/3 of recipe (as given in parentheses) for 1 pie —

Pig Hocks recipe

November 2, 1934. Henrietta Nesbitt Papers, Manuscript Division.

nov 2/34.

Boil with - Hot Pep. Onion - green - Pep cook until very tender Split & broil under Glaze

Melt - Butter - sauce with - lemon & salt chopped Parsley

(Pig Hocks) as President like them

Eleanor Roosevelt to Henrietta Nesbitt

July 26, 1937. Henrietta Nesbitt Papers, Manuscript Division.

VAL-KILL COTTAGES
HYDE PARK, DUTCHESS COUNTY
NEW YORK

July 26, 1937.

Dear Mrs. Nesbitt:

The President says that his dinners have been much better cooked. There are a few things that he thinks should be changed. For instance, he says that Sunday night when he and Miss Le Hand were alone, they had enough bacon and scrambled eggs for six people. I imagine that what happened was that you ordered sufficient in case there were a number of people and then of course, they did not use their own judgment in the kitchen when there were only two people.

I think if you would simply see that Ida or whoever is in the kitchen, used her own judgment when emergencies come up, either for less or more than you have ordered, and give her a little leeway in ordering, it will help.

The present arrangement seems to have worked very well so I would continue it and let Ida do her own buying of fresh foods. You order the things which you buy in quantity or keep on hand for emergencies. It will save you from running from one shop to I am so glad that we can keep her and I am writing her a line to that effect.

I was delighted to hear that you had your children with you and were going on a picnic. I wish you and Mr. Nesbitt could come up here for a few days sometime when the President is away. He says he will probably come up next Wednesday for several days. If he does, will you send Elizabeth, Reynolds or Mingo and Mrs. MacDuffie? Ask Elizabeth if she can get on without bringing any one else for the kitchen, but tell her that the kitchen maid is the only one in the house. The other people here are Robert, Jennings and one housemaid. Tell Mr. McIntyre several days before hand how many people will be coming up on the train.

I haven't had a chance to go on a picnic yet to use the new broiler but we are planning to do so very soon.

Affectionately,

Eleanor Roosevelt

Ruth Wakefield's Toll House Tried and True Recipes

 Ruth Graves Wakefield (1903–1977)

 New York: M. Barrows, second edition

 1938

 General Collections

TRIED AND TRUE RECIPES

Chocolate Cookies

Add
1 cup sugar to
½ cup melted fat and then
1 egg, beaten. Mix
1½ cups sifted flour and
½ tsp. soda and add alternating with
½ cup milk. Add
3 squares melted chocolate
¼ tsp. vanilla
¾ cup nuts and
¾ cup raisins

Drop from teaspoon on a baking dish and bake in a hot or 400° oven.

Chocolate Crunch Cookies

Cream
1 cup butter, add
¾ cup brown sugar
¾ cup granulated sugar and
2 eggs beaten whole. Dissolve
1 tsp. soda in
1 tsp. hot water, and mix alternately with
2¼ cups flour sifted with
1 tsp. salt. Lastly add
1 cup chopped nuts and
1 lb. Nestles yellow label chocolate, semi-sweet, which has been cut in pieces the size of a pea.
Flavor with
1 tsp. vanilla and drop half teaspoons on a greased cookie sheet. Bake 10 to 12 minutes in 375° oven. Makes 100 cookies.

Cocoanut Strips

Cut 2 slices of bread ¾ inch thick, remove crusts, then cut in strips ¾ inch wide. Put a small amount of sweetened condensed milk in a plate and ½ cup shredded cocoanut in another plate. Put strips in milk and cover, drain and cover with cocoanut. Toast on broiler until brown.

165

Among book collectors, obtaining the first edition is usually the object. Not so with Ruth Wakefield's *Toll House* cookbook. It's the 1938 second edition, seen here, containing the first chocolate chip cookie recipe, that attracts sweet-toothed bibliophiles. Wakefield, a former dietitian and home economics teacher, co-owned the extremely successful Toll House Inn in Whitman, Massachusetts. In one of the great moments in culinary history, while doing dream-job research concocting a new cookie to serve with ice cream, she mixed broken bits of Nestlé's chocolate bars into her dough, inventing the treat that the world had not yet realized it absolutely needed. The recipe appears here as Chocolate Crunch Cookies; "Toll House" was added to the name by 1940. Whatever it was called, demand for the recipe became so great that Wakefield reportedly licensed it to Nestlé for one dollar in exchange for a lifetime supply of chocolate. Although guests raved about Wakefield's traditional New England fare, it was her chocolate chip cookies that hit the nation's sweet spot and secured her legacy.

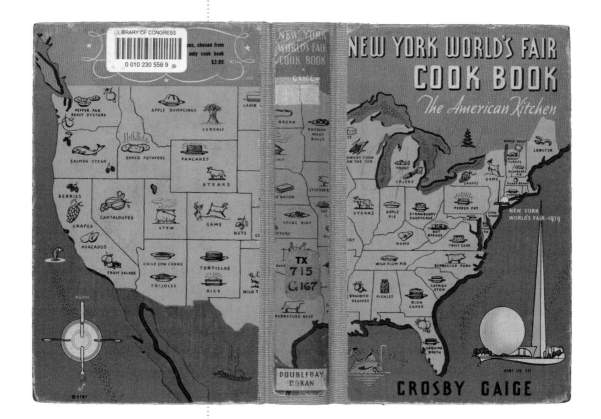

New York World's Fair Cook Book:

The American Kitchen

 Crosby Gaige (1882–1949)

 New York: Doubleday, Doran

 1939

 General Collections

Crosby Gaige, a Broadway producer, wrote this book ahead of the 1939 World's Fair in New York City. As the colorful map on the cover indicates, Gaige wanted to celebrate recipes from across America, some of which would be on offer at the fair. Recipes are divided regionally, followed by a list of menus from all forty-eight states, plus the then-territories of Alaska and Hawaii, as well as Puerto Rico. Gaige included a brief "acknowledgement to the first Native American cookery" explaining how indigenous peoples developed culinary uses of corn. "The cooks of America ought to raise their best stirring spoons in salute to this friendly standby," Gaige wrote.

New Trier Evening School Classes for Adults

Federal Art Project

Chicago: Illinois WPA Art Project, silkscreen poster

1941

Prints and Photographs Division

During the Great Depression, home economists, inspired by the scientific cooking movement at the turn of the century, promoted efficient and nutritious dietary adjustments that reflected the faltering economy. Such recommendations were taught in classes like the one advertised here in the Chicago suburb of New Trier. The US Department of Agriculture, specifically its Bureau of Home Economics, sponsored these classes, and along with the USDA's *Aunt Sammy's Radio Recipes*, they provided millions of Americans with economized meal suggestions, often featuring foodstuffs provided by government relief organizations.

How to Cook a Wolf

 M. F. K. Fisher (Mary Frances Kennedy) (1908–1992)

 New York: Duell, Sloan and Pearce

 1942

 General Collections

Alternately living in the United States and Europe, noted food author M. F. K. Fisher returned to America shortly before World War II broke out, just in time to write a cookbook that made the most of less in an era of blackouts, shortages, and ration books. (This cookbook is a distant cousin to the *Confederate Receipt Book*. For example, Fisher suggests placing in the oven "thinly sliced bread which is too stale to use any more. It makes good Melba toast.") Fisher took her title from Charlotte Gilman's poem "The Wolf at the Door," emphasizing common sense, multitasking, and culinary techniques to save money and stretch resources. She wrote engagingly of new alternatives for already existing food substitutes, balancing food nutrients by the day and not the meal, and enjoying "the pastime of seeing how many things you can cook at once in an oven." *New York Times* book reviewer Orville Prescott called her a "one-woman revolution in the field of literary cookery."

FIGHTING COOK & OTHER TROOPERS

ANZIO STEW

1 cow
brown gravy

2 rabbits (optional)

Get a cow anyway you can. Cut up cow in bite-size pieces which should take about 5 hours. Cover meat with brown gravy. Cook over gasoline fire about 4 hours.

If you need more meat, add the 2 rabbits, but only if necessary as most people do not like to find hare in their stew. Serves 350.

Nick De Gaeta
Staten Island, N.Y.

Anzio Stew, *from* Fighting Cook and Other Troopers

 Nick De Gaeta (1919–2015)

 Sol B. Weber Collection, Veterans History Project, American Folklife Center

In 1944, paratroopers Sol Weber and Nick De Gaeta, both of the 509th Parachute Infantry Battalion, each found themselves on their own after their planes missed the designated drop zones over Italy. Weber soon met up with about sixty other wandering paratroopers and, short on rations, had to improvise. "We ran into an ox," he recounted fifty years later. "We killed it, we singed it, we ate it. And we all got diarrhea. But it was food." De Gaeta, roaming about the countryside, was captured and briefly held by "friendlies" who initially mistook him for a German in unusual clothing. Long after the war, he contributed this recipe—apparently gleaned from personal experience—to the *Fighting Cook and Other Troopers* cookbook, a copy of which Weber kept with his wartime papers.

World War II Prisoner-of-War
Recipes and Cookbooks

ARMY CHOW, WHETHER MESS HALL GRUB, CANNED C-RATIONS, OR POUCHED MRES, HAS NEVER LACKED FOR EITHER SALT OR COMMENTARY. A MUCH LESSER-KNOWN ASPECT OF FEEDING AN ARMY ARE THE MANY POW RECIPES AND PERSONAL COOKBOOKS PRISONERS KEPT IN WHICH SOLDIERS IN THE THROES OF HUNGER SHARE RECIPES, JOT DOWN MEAL PLANS, AND MULL OVER WHAT THEY WILL EAT FIRST IF THEY EVER GET HOME.

During World War II, western Allied POWs held in Germany generally received adequate but monotonous potato- and sauerkraut-heavy rations supplemented with food delivered in Red Cross boxes. In the early months of 1945, however, as the end of the war drew near, conditions deteriorated and ravenous prisoners cobbled together what meals they could. Lt. Robert T. Booth, from New York and serving in the 87th Infantry Division, recalled that during his imprisonment in Limburg, "where we stayed and starved for a long time, food was the common subject of conversation. Men who had never been near a kitchen became gourmet chefs in their minds. They recited detailed recipes, described the fabulous dishes that they had made. . . . The camp 'library' (about 100 volumes) included a couple of cookbooks and some others that described meals in detail. Those books were in the strongest demand. It was hard to have a turn with one."

Meanwhile, in the Pacific Theater, Allied prisoners suffered from brutal treatment and starvation in Japanese-run POW camps throughout the war, with one out of three Americans dying while imprisoned. Kary Cadmus "K. C." Emerson, an army infantry officer from Oklahoma, survived the Bataan Death March in the Philippines and more than three years in captivity. In 1965, twenty years after the war ended, Emerson, who had remained in the army and become a renowned entomologist, wrote of his experiences and his wartime collection of international recipes: "Sooner or later every prisoner longs for food, dreams of food, and this becomes a major topic of discussion with others. Everyone has a favorite dish or meal, which he contributes to the discussion . . . and before long individuals start 'cookbooks' so that these dishes can be tried after the war." He noted that many of the recipes he and other inmates conjured up did not turn out to be as good as imagined when the former POWs tried making them once they returned home.

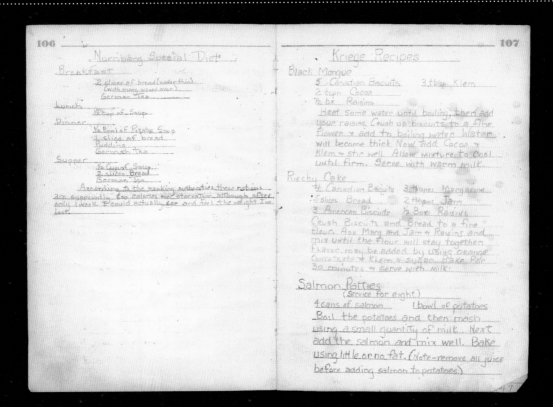

William Teller (1920-2013)

A Wartime Log, notebook pages 106-107, 1944-1945. Veterans History Project, American Folklife Center.

American POWs in Germany referred to themselves as "Kriegies," short for the German word for prisoner of war. Lt. William Teller, a Californian in the Army Air Forces, 783rd Bomber Squadron, kept a series of notebooks that detailed prison camp life, including a number of "Kriegie Recipes," such as Reichy Cake and Salmon Patties. Originally held in Stalag Luft III, he documented his meals almost daily, mentioning on January 23, 1945, that "tonight I'm making potato scallops, mashed potatoes, carrots, raisin pudding,

cream and coffee. I'm glad to be cook as it keeps one busy most of the day. I've used 3 different recipes in the last week and they [were] all good." Teller was later imprisoned in Nuremberg toward the end of the war. On the left page of his notebook, he provided the meager "Nurnberg Special Diet" prisoners endured. "I made a potato stew for dinner," he wrote on February 23. "Just potatoes and water plus bread. That is all we have left."

68.

SPAGHETTI (FRENCH) (6 people)

Brown 1" groundbeef in olive oil. Brown 1 large onion + 2 cloves garlic in butter. Mix above and add: 1 can tomatoe soup, 1¾ can tomatoe paste, and small can of mushrooms. Simmer 20 minutes. Boil ¾" spaghetti 20 minutes as in Italian. Place alternate layers of spaghetti + sauce/meat mix in baking dish. Sprinkle with cheese bake moderately 20 minutes + serve.

FRENCH APPLE BREAD - Mix 4 parts flour, 1 part apple pulp (warm). Add yeast. Beat well and let stand in southern jar 8-12 hrs. Mold in long. loaves + bake. Use very little water.

BLENTZA: Make 1" ball or cube cottage cheese. Dip in egg batter roll in corn meal. Fry, serve with sour cream.

BOWZA: 1½" meat scraps, 4 G. peppers, 2 onions, celery, carrots, etc. Mix chop together. Wrap 3 tbsp. of mix inside biscuit dough. Fry or use as dumplings.

AUSTRALIAN EGG PLANT: Slice egg plant. Squeeze out juice w/rolling pen. Dip in egg batter sprinkle w/ cheese + fry.

61.

ITALIAN SAUCE: Fry ½# hamburger, ¼# P. sausage in 1c. olive oil. Add 1c. water or wine, 1 sprig chopped parsley, 1c. chopped celery, 2 onions, 3 cloves garlic, ½# mushrooms. Stir till brown, add small can tomato paste, 2 can tomatoes, 1 tsp. turmeric, 2 sprigs rosemary, salt + pepper. Simmer ½ hr. Add ½c. sauterne wine. Add meat stock to proper thickness. or corn starch.

DUTCH PEA SOUP: Wash ½ pint dried peas and let soak overnite in cold water. Next morning let them simmer slowly for 2 hr. until thoroughly boiled. Then put sieve and add 2 pigs feet. Let boil one hour. Then take 500 grams of sausage (with many holes in sides) + cook together another ½ hr. Remove sausages. Then add salt, 4 leeks, handful of celery greens + 1 celery heart. In small pieces. Let boil on slow fire till meat separates from bones. Replace sausages. Serve hot but not lumpy. Sausages are eaten with soup.

FLATT BRÖD (Norg.) Oat flour mixed w/lard + milk into bread dough. Roll flat ½ thick + cook on top of stove. Then when brown, store until required. Place in damp cloth + when soft, cut into shapes, spread with butter + jam + roll.

LEFSE: Same only ¼ thick. Served cold.

K. C. Emerson (1918–1993)

Notebook 3, 1943–1944. K. C. Emerson Papers, Manuscript Division.

In neat legible script, K. C. Emerson recorded recipes he obtained from other imprisoned Allied officers in Zentsugi, Japan, during the winter of 1943–1944. "A diversity of items was included not because they were especially appealing, but because they were new to me and I felt that they could not be found later," he wrote. "Not being a good cook, I cannot guarantee that the receipts are good." These pages show entries for French-style spaghetti, Australian eggplant, Dutch pea soup, and Norwegian *flatt bröd*. Other recipes came from British, Javanese, New Zealander, and Russian POWs. Perhaps not surprisingly, fellow Americans contributed an abundance of barbecue sauce recipes.

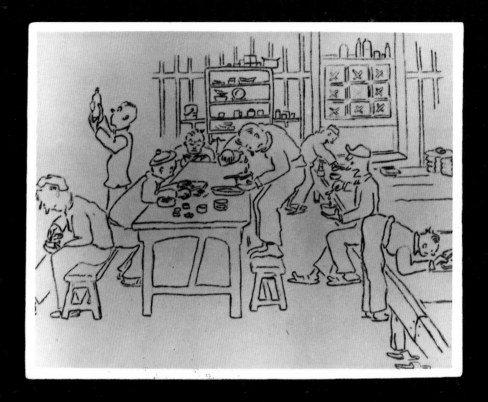

Kenneth G. Schacht (1913-1985)

Photograph of cartoon, ca. 1942–1945. K. C. Emerson Papers, Manuscript Division.

K. C. Emerson received this cartoon from fellow POW Kenneth George Schacht who documented their lives in a Japanese prison camp. It depicts prisoners eking out what little they can from their meager food allotment. An accompanying bit of doggerel read: "Some prisoners never seem to tire / Of building up a 'guanning' fire / They love to sit and blow and fan / Then cook up something in a can. / When there is no food in view / They even make plain water do."

Broda Rayborn
(1920–1980)

Diary page, January 28, 1945.
Veterans History Project, American Folklife Center.

Captured after the Battle of Corregidor in the Philippines, Staff Sergeant Broda Rayborn, of Idaho, serving in the 31st Infantry Division, was later shipped to Mukaishima prison camp in Hiroshima, Japan. In his diary he noted the recipe for a cake made using some of the items from the Red Cross parcels that POWs were entitled to receive. He also meticulously recorded the contents and "how these boxes will be used. 'Maybe.'" (Japanese officials rarely allowed boxes to be delivered, and those that arrived were treasured. Prison cooks usually took the ingredients from each box to make scant meals for the prisoners.) At the bottom of the page, Rayborn calculated how many "meals" could be obtained using milk, chocolate, jam, peanut butter, and cheese.

(red cross box)

January - 28 - 1945.

a cake Ike made from this issue of our 3 box's. Ike, Louie, myself. the red cross cake. with a little loot.

2 oz chese, 6 spoons P milk. ⅓ cup powdered beans. ⅓ can butter. ⅓ box raisins. ⅓ box sugar. ⅓ can jam. 1 chocolate bar. 1½ cup rice, barly flour. 1 spoon coffee. Yeast, Strawberry, ex. "Mix."

cream chese, milk, butter & sugar well. add raisins + beans meal add flour + yeast. mix thoroughly. divide mix into two equal parts in 1 part add 1 spoon coffee. in other add 1 spoon strawberry ex. Pour into papered ground pans - bake. "Icing" cream ⅓ can butter with ⅓ can jam for center filling. cream 1 bar choclate ⅓ can butter 3 spoons milk for outer icing. use plain creamed milk + butter for decorations, useing portion desired, coloring with straw berry + line. (color) choclate, Pink green + white) 2 layers 2" thick. weight 3 lbs.

(How these box's will be used.) "Maybe."

Meats)	(Dairy products)	(Sweets)	(Coffee)
3 Salmon	3 chese	3 Raisins	3 coffee.
3 Pate	3 milk powdered	6 choclate bars	
3 Spam	10 butter	3 Sugar	
3 corn buf.		3 jam	
2 Tang			
2 Luncheon meat.			

6 chocolate bars - 1 can milk - ½ lb. sugar = 15 meals
3 jam - 9 cans butter - ⅓ can milk = 12 meals
3 chese - 1 can milk - 1 butter = 10 meals

Now's the time for

JELL-O
BRAND
GELATIN DESSERT

SIX DELICIOUS FLAVORS

Having a little trouble, Mac? Buck up! You still can surprise the little woman and the kids with a swell Jell-O gelatin dessert! It's an absolute cinch to make . . . and we guarantee they'll love every bit of it!

JELL-O IS A REGISTERED TRADE-MARK OF GENERAL FOODS CORP.

Copr. 1952. General Foods Corp.

CHAPTER 4

"Anyone Can Cook"

THE POSTWAR KITCHEN AND BAR

During the mid-twentieth century, in the midst of the Cold War, the two leading superpowers in American cookbooks could not have been more different. Betty Crocker was a carefully crafted corporate character representing General Mills. Julia Child, whose real wartime career was in secret intelligence at the Office of Strategic Services, developed as her "first recipe" a repellant used to deter sharks from biting downed airmen or detonating undersea explosives. Their recipes for meatloaf, a dish that has come to represent the era, reflected their styles: fictional Betty used ten tasty but basic ingredients and non-fictional Julia called for nearly twice that, with an emphasis on seasoning. Despite the pair's differences, some cooks even pledged allegiance to both figures.

Throughout this period, publishers produced hundreds of cookbook titles aimed primarily at suburban women. Betty Crocker's brand-new and revised classic recipes were designed with modern electric appliances, red meat, and mass-produced boxed, canned, and frozen ingredients in mind. Those items were visibly prevalent in another significant postwar development—the well-stocked supermarket. Anyone who consumed green bean or tuna casserole and molded gelatin salads in the second half of the twentieth century could probably thank Betty. Meanwhile, Julia Child was teaching many of those same suburban women the art of French cooking through her enormously successful first cookbook and her many television shows.

With more Americans leaving rural areas and living on their own, a variety of cookbooks for singles or newlyweds on tight budgets appeared regularly. Cocktail recipe guides proliferated as well, as many households set up small bars or tables in their living rooms with the basic accoutrements of sophisticated beverage service.

The Fine Art of Mixing Drinks

David Embury
(1886–1960)

Garden City, NY:
Doubleday

1948

General Collections

By the mid-1940s, cocktails had become the purview of amateurs and hobbyists. David Embury was one such enthusiast, whose cocktail book became an instant classic. He went back to the basics, explaining "anyone can make good cocktails. The art of mixing drinks is no deep and jealously guarded secret." He divided cocktails generally into one of two categories: aromatic or sour; then listed ingredients for each cocktail by base, modifier, and special flavorings and coloring agents. The first chapter with recipes focuses on six American cocktails—the Martini, Manhattan, Old Fashioned, Daiquiri, Sidecar, and Jack Rose—knowledge of which, Embury wrote, would allow a host "to stand much higher in the regard of his guests than will the indiscriminate chop-suey dispenser who throws together a little of everything." Mixologist and cocktail historian Derek Brown has described the book as a modern cocktail bible, the "New Testament" to Jerry Thomas's "Old Testament."

How to Cook and Eat in Chinese

Buwei Yang Chao (1889–1981)

New York: John Day

1945

General Collections

Not many authors lead off with "I am ashamed to have written this book" as Buwei Yang Chao did. "First, because I am a doctor and ought to be practicing instead of cooking. Secondly, because I didn't write the book." Having moved from China to New York in 1938, and at the urging of friends, she produced the first cookbook of its kind, presenting genuine Chinese recipes written in English. Her husband and daughter translated and edited her Chinese manuscript, arguing over English usage versus imitating Mandarin phrasing, hence her reticence to claim authorship. One upshot of the ordeal was the invention of the term "stir-fry." In detailed and thoughtful sections, Chao addresses the Chinese approach to food, meal preparation, and etiquette. "Good cooking consists in making the best use of the eating material," she said. "The cooking materials should only enhance the natural taste of the eating material and not take its place." Nobel laureate Pearl S. Buck, the best-known American to know about China best, contributed a rave review in the book's preface, wishing she could give the Nobel Peace Prize to Chao for her "contribution to international understanding."

La Bonne Cuisine:
Four Recipes for Voice and Piano

Leonard Bernstein (1918–1990)

1947

Leonard Bernstein Collection, Music Division

Celebrated American composer and conductor Leonard Bernstein wrote this song cycle for piano and voice based on a French cookbook he owned. In 1947, he adapted four recipes from *La Bonne Cuisine Française* (1899) by Emile Dumont into poems and then set them to music. The piece premiered in 1948 in New York City with pianist Edwin McArthur accompanying the mezzo-soprano Marion Bell. The next year Bernstein recorded it with himself at piano and Jennie Tourel, the piece's dedicatee, singing. In addition to the plum pudding recipe depicted in the holograph score above, Bernstein adapted the cooking instructions for Rabbit at Top Speed, Ox Tails, and Tavouk Gueunksis, a Turkish milk pudding made with chicken. Ahead of a 1977 performance of *La Bonne Cuisine*, the *New York Times* admitted, "Food buffs are bound to be frustrated, considering the abbreviated and incomplete recipes." Despite not listing all the ingredients for each dish, the concert was "worthwhile just to see and hear the expressions of the baritone as he goes into raptures over the Tavouk Gueunksis."

A Date with a Dish: *A Cook Book of American Negro Recipes*

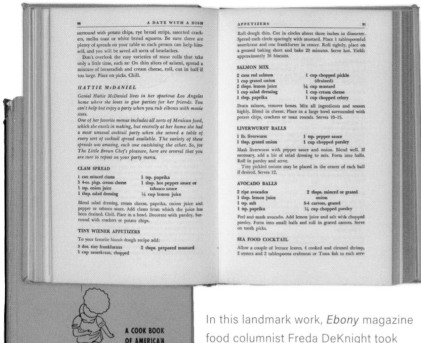

Freda DeKnight (1909–1963)

New York: Hermitage Press

1948

General Collections

In this landmark work, *Ebony* magazine food columnist Freda DeKnight took readers on an unprecedented nationwide exploration of black culture through cooking and cuisine. *Date with a Dish* refuted the notion that African-American cookery was solely a Southern convention, as DeKnight, who spent time with hundreds of "chefs and home cooks" in her travels, shared their recipes, anecdotes, histories, pro tips, and innovations. The head chef of Philadelphia's renowned Holland Caterers, an Iowa mother of twelve, a Michigan chef with the Grand Trunk Railroad, various celebrities (Louis Armstrong, Lena Horne, Hattie McDaniel), and many others warranted her close attention. "I was thrilled at the many new methods of preparing fish I had the good fortune of learning while visiting colored families and friends who live in and about coastal areas," wrote DeKnight. "Many could not afford more than occasional meat dishes, and fish necessarily became one of their main standbys. They had a way of marinating fish in citric juices, garlic, herbs, and onions that made fish seem more than fish." She also mixed in her own menus and recipes, charming readers with her conversational tone and commentary from her literary alter-ego, the "Little Brown Chef," seen taking a bow on the book's cover. Although "the recipes in this book have been tested for the average cook to master," others were specifically value-added, as when she pointed to "a few menus that are sure to dazzle the gang and get that extra kiss or diamond bracelet you are working on."

Fit for Print, Banned for Broadcast

WHEN PROHIBITION ENDED IN 1933, THE PARTY PICKED UP WHERE IT HAD LEFT OFF FOR THE BEER AND WINE BUSINESS, BUT THE LIQUOR INDUSTRY RESTRAINED ITSELF. REGARDED BY TEMPERANCE ORGANIZATIONS AS THE MOST DANGEROUS AND GREATEST OF THREE EVILS, LIQUOR WAS SUBJECT TO STRICT REGULATIONS IN HOW AND WHERE IT WAS SOLD. THOSE PROMOTING SPIRITS, FEARFUL OF ATTRACTING NEGATIVE ATTENTION OR SETTING OFF PROHIBITION 2.0, VOLUNTARILY HELD BACK ON SOME FORMS OF ADVERTISING, LEST "DRY" ADVOCATES OR THEIR CONGRESSIONAL REPRESENTATIVES THREATEN THEIR BUSINESS.

In 1936, liquor producers agreed not to advertise their products on the radio, a policy they applied twelve years later to television, and the pact held together until 1996. Instead, they focused on print and outdoor advertising, primarily in magazines, newspapers, and billboards. In the meantime, pioneering ad design and improvements in photography and printing perfectly suited the way liquor could be presented. Gleaming bottles and glasses filled with warm or sparkling potables popped off the page, and liquor producers poured money into high-end design and big-name advertising agencies.

Postwar prosperity unabashedly affected American lifestyles and pricier drink options, and ads presented liquor as a sophisticated accoutrement to the worldly household and as the obvious beverage of choice for the discerning consumer. During the golden age of advertising that began in the 1960s, the liquor industry had a lock on stylish ads, and as the Fleischmann's piece seen on page 79 shows, that was something to sniff at.

Please, Oh Please, Don't Smother Our Flavor!

White Rock Water. Time, *June 10, 1935.*

Drawn from the springs—frequented by the indigenous Potawatomi for its medicinal benefits—in what became the spa town of Waukesha, Wisconsin, White Rock Water promoted its product as a naturally lithiated and carbonated mixer that would enhance various whiskies.

Warm Welcome

Three Feathers Reserve Whiskies. Esquire, *March 1947.*

This 1947 ad from Three Feathers plays on the reader's sense of hospitality, advertising that its whiskey will make guests flock to the drink maker's door. Hot toddies are often served in cold weather to warm up the drinker, and this ad subtly uses snow to inspire a wintery feel.

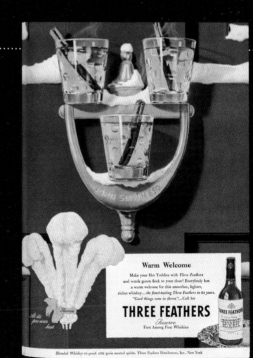

Gilbey's Gin

Gilbey's Distilled London Dry Gin. Life, *March 31, 1958.*

Gilbey's promoted its product as urbane and international. The small print of this ad noted it was distilled and bottled at more than a dozen locations in Africa, Europe, and North and South America.

Six New Twists on Old Fashioned Hospitality with Hiram Walker's Cordials

Hiram Walker. Sports Illustrated, *October 31, 1960.*

This advertisement featuring a Mint Frappe, Brandy Alexander, Comrade Kelly, Alexander's Sister, Blackberry Frappe, and Sidecar came with simple recipes using Hiram Walker's cordials. In the long-running "Rainbow of Distinctive Flavors" campaign, readers could order a ten-cent copy of a *Compleat Cordial Cookery and Cocktail Guide* with ideas for successful entertaining and new drink and dish recipes, making a cosmopolitan lifestyle all the more accessible.

Sniff It Like It Is Right on This Page

Fleischmann's Distilled Dry Gin.
Esquire, *September 1969.*

In an early application of scratch-and-sniff technology, Fleichsmann's used a small fragrant pad in its print ad that delivered a convincing aroma of juniper berries and still suggests a Martini scent more than a half century after it was produced.

Sniff it like it is right on this page

Scratch the tape then sniff the tape for the world's driest martini

Back in 1870, Fleischmann developed America's first dry gin. We still make the driest.
To tempt you to try it, we've even taped the scent of a Fleischmann's martini right on this

page. Just scratch this piece of tape and sniff it.
We hope that once you have taken a whiff of our martini, you won't be satisfied until you have a taste. Then you'll be extremely satisfied.

Fleischmann's. The world's driest gin since 1870
THE FLEISCHMANN DISTILLING CORPORATION NYC 90 PROOF DISTILLED FROM AMERICAN GRAIN

Betty Crocker's Picture Cook Book

 General Mills

 Minneapolis: General Mills

 1950

General Collections

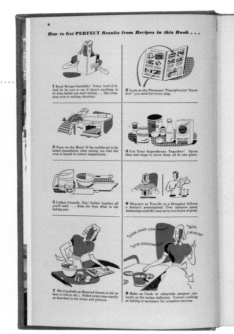

Betty Crocker promoted time- and money-saving packaged soup and baking mixes, but she herself was made from scratch. Her first name was meant to evoke a friendly neighbor lady, her last name was borrowed from a well-liked former company director, and her face, as seen in her first official painted portrait (1936), was a composite of various women who worked for her creator, General Mills. Beginning in 1921 "Betty" appeared in magazine ads, then on radio and television programs—in 1997 she would get her own website—and corresponded for decades with the nation's homemakers at the rate of two thousand letters a day. Her enormous archive of mail detailed exactly what it was her millions of adherents wanted to know about cooking, and her ultimate fact-filled response was a landmark tome that dramatically changed what a cookbook could be. With Betty's affable tone, a thousand photographs and step-by-step illustrations, useful easy-to-read reference charts, and more than two thousand simplified and endlessly tested recipes, the book gifted readers with all the basics and "first choice" meals the home cook could ever need . . . until the next edition.

Mrs. Warren's Devil's Food Cake

ca. 1950

Earl Warren Papers,
Manuscript Division

While serving as the fourteenth chief justice of the United States, Earl Warren received dozens of requests for recipes. These requests came from charities, hospitals, and other organizations looking to auction off recipe books or authors publishing celebrity cookbooks. A third type of request often came from amateur recipe hunters, a fad at the time. Similar to autograph seekers, these hobbyists wrote to public figures hoping to get insight into their regular cooking habits. Regardless of the requestor, Warren would send this recipe for devil's food cake from his Swedish-born wife, the former Nina Meyers. When a reporter asked if the chief justice enjoyed cooking, his secretary replied, "The chief justice does not cook."

Supreme Court of the United States
Washington 25, D. C.

MRS. WARREN'S DEVIL'S FOOD CAKE

CHAMBERS OF
THE CHIEF JUSTICE

1/4 lb. butter or substitute	2 cups sifted cake flour
1 cup granulated sugar	1 tsp. baking soda
1 cup brown sugar	Pinch of salt
3 squares Baker's bitter chocolate (melted)	
6 egg yolks	1 tsp. vanilla
3 tablespoons cold water	1 cup buttermilk

Cream butter and sugar thoroughly and add melted chocolate. Add egg yolks, which have been beaten well with the water. Sift together 3 times the flour, soda, and salt. Add to first mixture alternately with the buttermilk until all used. Add vanilla. Beat until well mixed. Bake in two large layer tins (1 1/2 inches deep x 9 inches) for about 35 minutes in 350 degree oven.

Use a seven-minute frosting between layers, and chocolate frosting on top and sides.

Seven-Minute Frosting

2 egg whites	1 1/2 cups gran. sugar	5 tablespoons
1 tsp. vanilla	1 1/2 tsp. Karo light syrup	cold water

Put above ingredients, except vanilla, in top of double boiler. Beat with egg beater (over boiling water) for 7 minutes, or until mixture stands up in peaks. Remove from fire and add vanilla.

Chocolate Frosting

To 1 lb. confectioner's sugar, add 1/2 cup cocoa, pinch of salt, and 1 tsp. vanilla. Have strong coffee for the liquid, about 1/3 cup, and add enough to make the mixture of the right consistency to spread. Add 2 tbs. melted butter just before frosting the cake. Spread on top and sides -- sprinkle with chopped walnuts, or chopped assorted salted nuts.

Recipe for
Featherlite Pancakes

 Rosa Parks (1913–2005)

 undated

 Rosa Parks Papers, Manuscript Division

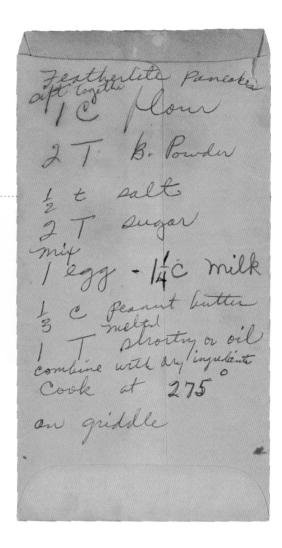

Revered as a civil rights icon, Rosa Parks regularly made notes, lists, and drafts on whatever paper was available, including this manila envelope where she recorded a pancake recipe. The key ingredient: one-third cup of melted peanut butter. Growing up on a farm in rural Alabama, Parks mastered basic cooking at age six. After refusing to give up her bus seat to a white passenger in 1955, she became a household name during the Montgomery Bus Boycott. She later oversaw the dining room and housekeeping staff at the Holly Tree Inn in Hampton, Virginia. Parks was a vegetarian before it was fashionable, favoring broccoli, greens, sweet potatoes, and green beans. The author of several books, she hoped to one day write a healthy lifestyle cookbook, and although that never happened, she credited her long life to a nutritious diet that also made room for dessert.

HASCHICH FUDGE
(which anyone could whip up on a rainy day)

This is the food of Paradise—of Baudelaire's Artificial Paradises: it might provide an entertaining refreshment for a Ladies' Bridge Club or a chapter meeting of the DAR. In Morocco it is thought to be good for warding off the common cold in damp winter weather and is, indeed, more effective if taken with large quantities of hot mint tea. Euphoria and brilliant storms of laughter; ecstatic reveries and extensions of one's personality on several simultaneous planes are to be complacently expected. Almost anything Saint Theresa did, you can do better if you can bear to be ravished by '*un évanouissement reveillé.*'

Take 1 teaspoon black peppercorns, 1 whole nutmeg, 4 average sticks of cinnamon, 1 teaspoon coriander. These should all be pulverised in a mortar. About a handful each of stoned dates, dried figs, shelled almonds and peanuts: chop these and mix them together. A bunch of *canibus sativa* can be pulverised. This

260 *The Alice B. Toklas Cook Book*

along with the spices should be dusted over the mixed fruit and nuts, kneaded together. About a cup of sugar dissolved in a big pat of butter. Rolled into a cake and cut into pieces or made into balls about the size of a walnut, it should be eaten with care. Two pieces are quite sufficient.

Obtaining the *canibus* may present certain difficulties, but the variety known as *canibus sativa* grows as a common weed, often unrecognised, everywhere in Europe, Asia and parts of Africa; besides being cultivated as a crop for the manufacture of rope. In the Americas, while often discouraged, its cousin, called *canibus indica*, has been observed even in city window boxes. It should be picked and dried as soon as it has gone to seed and while the plant is still green.

The Alice B. Toklas Cook Book

 Alice B. Toklas (1877–1967)

 New York: Harper & Row

 1984 reprint, first published in 1954

 General Collections

In this literary cookbook, Alice B. Toklas, who with Gertrude Stein maintained a bohemian salon at their Paris home, shared her reminiscences, her own French and American recipes, and contributions from the luminaries she co-hosted. The original 1954 British edition included a recipe for Haschich Fudge, but the American edition did not. Toklas, who obtained the recipe from avant-garde artist Brion Gysin, failed to notice that it called for "a bunch of *canibus sativa*" when she added it to her manuscript. Her American publisher, unsure if it should run this "dangerous" recipe, inexplicably sought guidance from the White House. The Eisenhower administration merely replied that anyone could make the fudge, but they could not legally consume it. (The fudge was not actually fudge, but rather *majoun*, a Moroccan candy.) Although later American editions, such as this thirtieth anniversary reprint, reinstated the famous "fudge," the film *I Love You, Alice B. Toklas!* (1968), starring Peter Sellers, compounded the erroneous belief that the censored recipe had been for pot brownies.

Profit and Weight Loss

IN THE HISTORY OF DIETING, WHICH DATES BACK TO ANTIQUITY, WILLIAM THE CONQUEROR IS SAID TO HAVE PUT HIMSELF ON AN ALCOHOL-ONLY MEAL PLAN ONCE HE BECAME TOO LARGE TO RIDE HIS HORSE. AMERICANS LATER LED THE WAY IN OFFBEAT DIETING WITH THE HOLLYWOOD DIET (ALSO KNOWN AS THE GRAPEFRUIT DIET), THE SEVEN-DAY CABBAGE SOUP DIET, AND THE MISNAMED ISRAELI ARMY DIET. AS THE PUBLIC GREW HEAVIER, COOKBOOKS DRAMATICALLY SHIFTED IN TONE AND CONTENT IN THE 1960S AND 1970S. IN AN ONSLAUGHT OF BESTSELLING WORKS, AUTHORS NOT ONLY ADDRESSED DIETING, BUT INTERCONNECTED TOPICS, INITIATING AND DOCUMENTING NATIONAL CONVERSATIONS ON PROCESSED FOOD, JUNK FOOD, FITNESS, ENVIRONMENTALISM, AND EATING YOUR VEGETABLES. REPRESENTATIVE TITLES FROM THIS ERA INCLUDE *LET'S COOK IT RIGHT* (1962), *MEATLESS MEALS* (1966), *THE ART OF SALAD MAKING* (1968), *COUNT YOUR CALORIES* (1970), AND *FOREVER THIN* (1970), CREATING AN ARRAY OF COOKBOOK SUBGENRES THAT REMAINS ROBUST.

Dr. Atkins' Diet Revolution: *The High Calorie Way to Stay Thin Forever*

Robert C. Atkins (1930–2003), recipes and menus by Fran Gare and Helen Monica. New York: D. McKay, 1972. General Collections.

Fad diets come and go, perhaps none as regularly as the literally against-the-grain, low-carbohydrate regimen Dr. Robert C. Atkins prescribed in his eponymous bestselling book. The first and subsequent revised editions sold more than 15 million copies, making it one of the most successful titles in American history. Atkins, a cardiologist, argued that burning fat rather than glucose would shed pounds. His method's original plan allowed for an initial high-fat diet of nearly unlimited helpings of steak, bacon, eggs, and cheese but no fruit, bread, or grains. The controversial book launched low-carb food trends, and "doing Atkins" has occasionally resurged in popularity in the decades after the book came out, notably in 2002, prompting *Time* magazine to name the author one of its "Persons of the Year." Menus and more than one hundred recipes are included, one being for Illegal, But Not Immoral or Fattening Cheese Cake.

Shed Pounds with Cocktails and Gourmet Fare

Jane (1922–2003) and Kent Voss (1920–1998), New York: Pocket Books, 1965. General Collections.

Published a year after the landmark Surgeon General's report confirmed the toxic effects of tobacco use, this cookbook offers "a diet designed for those who have stopped smoking and need a weight-control method which requires the absolute minimum of will power." It was also aimed at middle-aged folks of indeterminate will power. Like many earlier weight-loss diets, this one stressed a low-carbohydrate approach but was designed to satisfy aspiring or modestly sophisticated palates on moderate budgets. Dieters could choose from a month's worth of menus with recipes ranging from artichokes with Hollandaise sauce to zucchini casserole.

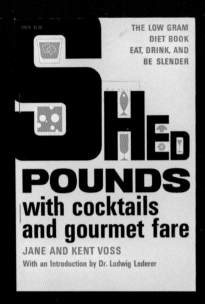

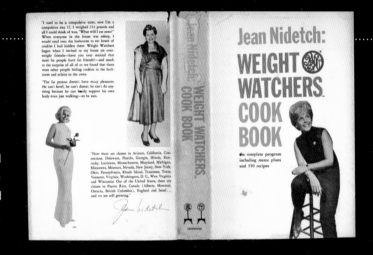

Weight Watchers' Cook Book

Jean Nidetch (1923–2015), New York: Hearthside Press, 1966. General Collections.

The Weight Watchers local group program that gained an international following and became a global empire began in Jean Nidetch's humble apartment ("furnished in early poverty," as she put it) in Queens, New York. The forty friends and friends-of-friends who crammed into her living room sought a supportive alternative to fad dieting, and Nidetch officially founded Weight Watchers, Inc., in 1963. Its restrictive high-protein, low-calorie diet plan came by way of the New York Bureau of Nutrition, which Nidetch transformed into a highly influential cookbook filled with simple recipes, anecdotes, and advice. The regimen emphasized abstention over moderation; it prohibited meal skipping, alcohol, sweets, and fatty foods. To the dismay of her publisher, Nidetch took an unusual approach to promoting her cookbook by urging people not to buy it, at least not until they got the hang of her program. It went on to sell 1.5 million copies.

The Best of Taste:
The Finest Food of Fifteen Nations

 SACLANT-NATO Cookbook Committee

 Annapolis, MD: US Naval Institute

 1957

 General Collections

Less than a decade after the founding of the North Atlantic Treaty Organization, the multinational military alliance created this cookbook, whose proceeds went to the NATO Scholarship and Fellowship Fund. SACLANT—short for Supreme Allied Commander Atlantic—was the main American branch of NATO, based in Norfolk, Virginia, under Rear Admiral Jerauld Wright. The wives of the SACLANT officers collected menus, recipes, and culinary treasures from a variety of NATO members, as well as favorite dishes from the leaders of member nations— such as President Dwight Eisenhower's recipe for beef stew.

"I'm a children's book editor. It's fun—fun—fun. I work in a big office. It's *so big.* . . ."

ESQUIRE : *August*

"I'm a Children's Book Editor"

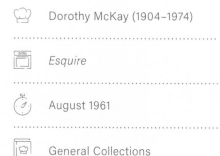

Dorothy McKay (1904–1974)

Esquire

August 1961

General Collections

Dorothy McKay was known for her colorful and humorous cartoons in publications such as *Esquire*, the *Saturday Evening Post*, *Life*, and *Collier's*. By 1961, when this cartoon appeared in *Esquire*, the cocktail party was a common form of American socializing. The first written record of a "cocktail party" was in St. Louis in 1917.

Ironically, Prohibition helped maintain its popularity because, without access to public bars, drinking in homes became more common. Later, with the rise of amateur mixology, cocktail parties became the dominant mode of at-home social gatherings in many urbane households.

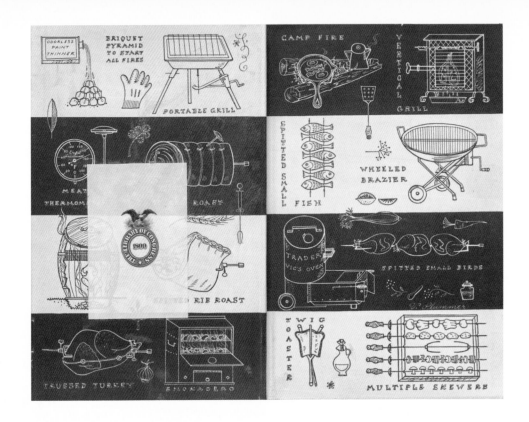

The Complete Book of Outdoor Cookery

 Helen Evans Brown (1904–1964)
and James A. Beard (1903–1985)

 Garden City, NY: Doubleday

 1955

 General Collections

With only a syllable's difference in their titles, these two works staked claims as the definitive word on barbecues, cookouts, and picnics, bookending a mid-century shift from the dining room to the patio. In an era of postwar prosperity and new suburban neighborhoods, *Popular Mechanics* reported in 1956 that "From Maine to California and from Minnesota to Alabama, thousands of families are taking up outdoor living for many months of the year. Patios, eating areas, places for play and relaxation are transforming back yards throughout the nation." Acclaimed food columnist Helen Evans Brown and her then lesser-known collaborator, James

Barbecue Books, Well Done

The Complete Book of Outdoor Cooking

 Janell Webster, editor

 Montgomery, AL: Favorite Recipes Press

 1970

 General Collections

of equipment and recipes. Beard—who soon became a towering culinary figure and the namesake of a foundation that gives out prestigious awards in gastronomy—received top billing in later editions. By 1970, cookbooks for campers and amateur grill masters were plentiful and often indistinguishable when Favorite Recipes Press set new aspirational standards for backyard entertaining with its artfully staged full-color photography in Janell Webster's lavishly illustrated volume.

Beard, noticed this too: "In recent years all America has become enchanted with outdoor cookery . . . but most of all we marvel at the flavor of the food." Authoritative and instructive, Brown and Beard covered a panoply

Mastering the Art of French Cooking

Julia Child (1912–2004), Louisette Bertholle (1905–1999), and Simone Beck (1904–1991)

New York: Knopf

1961

General Collections

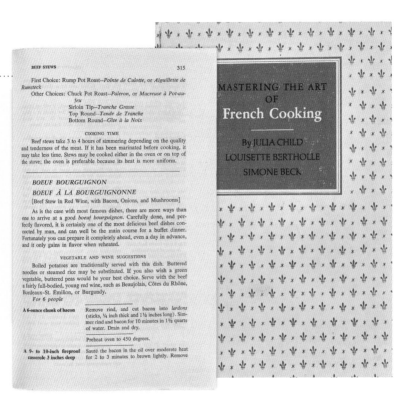

"Anyone can cook in the French manner," Julia Child declared in the foreword to the first edition of *Mastering the Art of French Cooking*. Child and her coauthors demystified French cuisine for millions, specifically "the servantless American cook." Similar to *The Joy of Cooking*, every recipe clearly lists the ingredients, which run vertically to the left of the directions. Also included are sections on kitchen equipment, definitions of French terms, and various chopping methods, while twenty-five illustrations help the reader understand difficult techniques. Child had learned many of these recipes while enrolled in the famous cooking school Le Cordon Bleu in Paris, where her husband Paul was stationed while working for the State Department.

To promote the book, Child demonstrated how to make an omelet on Boston public television station WGBH. Her live cooking was an immediate hit, and WGBH invited Child to create an entire show in 1962. Having just purchased her first television set, Child fully embraced the idea, resulting in more than two hundred episodes of *The French Chef*. The first non-pilot episode featured beef bourguignon from the recipe shown here. Child was inviting and gregarious and did not edit out mistakes, endearing herself to legions of culinary-minded Americans.

Single Girl's Cookbook

 Helen Gurley Brown (1922–2012)

 New York: Bernard Geis Associates

 1969

 General Collections

Saucepans and the Single Girl

 Jinx Kragen and Judy Perry

 Garden City, NY: Doubleday

 1965

 General Collections

chapter 11

In her 1962 bestselling book *Sex and the Single Girl*, Helen Gurley Brown encouraged bachelorettes to seek and enjoy their independence. Capitalizing on the famous title, former Stanford University roommates Jinx Kragen and Judy Perry aimed their good-natured *Saucepans and the Single Girl* at young career women who are "suddenly stranded in the kitchen." The recipes are intentionally easy on paychecks, given that the authors figured on a budget that allotted $200 monthly for clothes but only $10 for food—hence an entry for Humbleburger Soup. Despite her lack of expertise in the kitchen, Brown, the editor-in-chief of *Cosmopolitan*, produced her own cookbook, offering a reliable resource that delved deeply into entertaining, especially the well-orchestrated cocktail party. She suggests inviting "too many people. Way too many. . . . If a man gets his hands up to light a cigarette and can't get them down again because there isn't any room, that's about the right number of people."

Cooking Terms

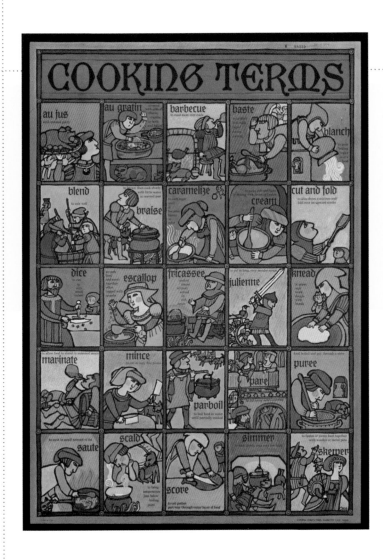

 Jane Oka

 Sausalito, CA: Portal Publications, Photomechanical print

 1969

 Prints and Photographs Division

This striking print uses medieval cartoon figures to depict a variety of cooking terms. A figure pouring boiling water from a turret demonstrates blanching; another brandishes a longsword to demonstrate julienning. And a besotted courtier demonstrates "marinate" by drinking his own seasoned sauce—wine. The poster was used as set dressing in a 1977 episode of the sitcom *Three's Company*, appearing on the main trio of roommates' refrigerator.

"There's a Man in My Kitchen"

EARLY PRINTED COOKBOOKS WERE AIMED AT UPPER CLASS WHITE WOMEN. TITLES SUCH AS *THE GOOD HUSWIFES JEWELL* (1585) AND *THE ENGLISH HUS-WIFE* (1615) IMPLIED A FEMALE READERSHIP, ALBEIT A WEALTHY ONE. SIMILAR TITLES APPEARED IN THE EIGHTEENTH AND NINETEENTH CENTURIES; THE FIRST COOKBOOK PRINTED ON AMERICAN SOIL WAS A 1742 REPRINT OF *THE COMPLEAT HOUSEWIFE*, ORIGINALLY WRITTEN IN LONDON IN 1727 BY ELIZA SMITH.

In the decades after the American Revolution, the traditional gendered stratification of labor meant that men worked outside the home while women focused on domestic duties. This trend continued in the United States for most of the nineteenth century as well. As a result, while professional chefs at restaurants, hotels, and the like were almost exclusively men, cookbooks targeted women who cooked or supervised the cooking in their homes. Beginning in the 1920s, publishers began producing cookbooks that catered specifically to men, a trend that continues well into the twenty-first century. These books—with titles like *For Men Only* (1937), *That Man in the Kitchen* (1946), or *Fearless Cooking for Men* (1977)—relayed similar messages that men can cook just like women can. The books found a market, albeit a niche one. By 1957, an article in *Ladies Home Journal* titled "There's a Man in my Kitchen" indicated that more than 70 percent of men cooked at least somewhat occasionally.

The Stag Cookbook: *Written for Men by Men*

Carroll McCoy Sheridan (1889–1924), New York: George H. Doran, 1922. Rare Book and Special Collections Division.

Carroll Sheridan collected recipes from male celebrities, utilizing their popularity to reinforce the notion that men could cook successfully. Participants included politicians (president Warren Harding gave his waffle recipe), authors (Stephen Vincent Benet: Macaroni Stew), actors (Charlie Chaplin: Steak and Kidney Pie), and composers (John Philip Sousa: Pelotas a la Spaghetti). Written during Prohibition, the cookbook includes several cheeky remarks making fun of the ban on alcohol. One recipe for preparing terrapin states that "If pre-Prohibition sherry is not available, names and addresses of seventy-one bootleggers can be supplied." Due to such quips, one reviewer described the book as "an amusing—and also delectably instructive—novelty in the way of cookbooks."

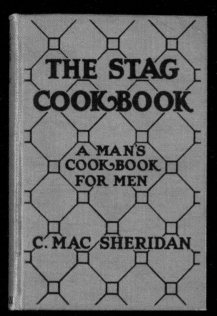

The Best Men Are Cooks

Frank Shay (1888–1954), New York: Coward-McCann, 1941. General Collections.

This cookbook, which appeared on the eve of America's entry into World War II, reflected a common theme of midcentury male-oriented cookbooks that men could cook whatever they wanted, and as well as women could. In his preface, Frank Shay explained that he wrote the book because "women have reduced cooking to a science while men cooks are working to restore it to its former high estate as one of the finer arts." This recipe for Jambalaya Damnyankee typifies the stereotypical hearty "male" recipes Shay

JAMBALAYA DAMNYANKEE

In Louisiana and along the Gulf Coast, there is no excuse for any jambalaya other than the genuine McCoy. But as long as Uncle Sam insists that other parts of the country be populated, it is impossible for all of us to emigrate to the Jambalaya Belt. The writer has long been insulting Creole cuisine by calling the following a jambalaya and getting away with it.

2 cups hot boiled rice	1 cup chicken stock, or 1
½ pound boiled ham	can condensed chicken
1 can wet-pack shrimp	soup
1 onion, minced	1 tablespoon bacon fat
Salt and pepper	

Sauté the diced ham and onion in the bacon fat until nicely browned. Add well-drained rice, seasonings, and chicken stock, simmer for a few minutes, then add the cleaned shrimps and cook until the shrimps are hot.

included. Ironically, wartime rationing would soon make many of these recipes difficult, despite Shay's optimistic insistence that "nowhere in the world is there a country with culinary resources comparable to those of America

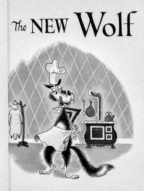

The New Wolf in Chef's Clothing:
The Picture Cook and Drink Book for Men

Robert H. Loeb Jr. (1913–1996), Chicago: Follett, 1958. General Collections.

In his introduction to the original 1950 edition, Robert H. Loeb Jr., wrote, "the purpose of this book is to enfranchise the male... he can become a gustatory eagle, king of the kitchen, and baron of the bar." The other purpose, Loeb explained, was to woo women with successful cooking. With a wolf-dressed-as-chef as a guide, the cookbook exudes simplicity with step-by-step illustrations instead of written recipes. The approach proved popular; in addition to this 1958 reprint, the book was reissued in 2000.

Man with a Pan: *Culinary Adventures of Fathers Who Cook for Their Families*

John Donohue, ed., Chapel Hill, NC: Algonquin Books of Chapel Hill, 2011. General Collections.

For this compendium, John Donohue collected recipes from fathers, mostly literary figures, including novelist Stephen King and food writer Mark Bittman. Each author's section has the same ingredients: a brief essay explaining their history with food and cooking; a few recipes; and a commentary on their favorite cookbooks and food-related writing. Unlike in earlier male-focused cookbooks, there is less emphasis on "manliness" and more on familial duty. Donohue, a *New Yorker* editor, peppers the book with culinary cartoons from the magazine.

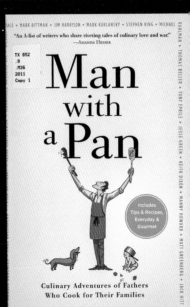

Dining al Fresco: *The Wolf Trap Picnic Cookbook*

 Photo by Renée Comet

 Vienna, VA: Wolf Trap Associates

 1992

General Collections

CHAPTER 5

"A Flavor Revolution"

GOING GREEN AND GLOBAL

A perusal of late twentieth-century cookbooks reveals a smorgasbord of classic, innovative, and offbeat offerings. Old standbys remained in print or were updated, including Fannie Farmer's 1896 *Boston School of Cooking*, *The Joy of Cooking*, and a multitude of Betty Crocker titles. Magazine mainstays such as *Better Homes and Gardens*, *Good Housekeeping*, *Southern Living*, and *Sunset* put out cookbooks as well. At the same time, some Americans were cooking faster than ever in their new microwave ovens or were taking a stab at other food trends that called for more specialized cookbooks, as the public experimented with vegetarianism, pasta, crêpes, and fondue. The cocktail revival, following a lull in the 1970s and 1980s, renewed similar interest in old drink manuals as "bartender historians" consulted original texts and posted recipes online.

Although major publishers continued to feature traditional, regional, and multicultural cookbooks, the advent of "desktop publishing" and an increase in small presses made possible a greater number of do-it-yourself cookbooks from lower-profile chefs and aspiring Martha Stewarts. Large publishing houses took notice, funneling a wide variety of local, farm-to-table, and unorthodox cookbooks into the mainstream. Meanwhile, cooking shows, once the province of public television, migrated to cable and attracted large, devoted audiences. In 1993, the launch of the Food Network catapulted some of those previously lesser-known chefs to celebrity status, including Emeril Lagasse and Paula Dean. For star chefs, publishing cookbooks is an essential part of personal branding and multimedia exposure.

The concept of comfort food and culinary nostalgia took hold and found expression in home-style, heritage, and retro cookbooks, dovetailing neatly with the movement toward self-help and self-care. The sushi craze centered in California spread eastward, and cuisine from beyond Mexico to the farthest reaches of Latin America landed on tables throughout the United States. Inventive fusion cuisines mixed flavors and ingredients, and America, long regarded as a "melting pot," took that description to a new and literal level.

The Vegetarian Epicure

 Anna Thomas (b. 1948)

 New York: Knopf

 1972

 General Collections

As a UCLA film school student, far from the red carpet, Anna Thomas created a classic cookbook whose phenomenal success funded her education and later cinematic projects. *The Vegetarian Epicure* grew out of low-budget necessity, but one that substituted joy for the drabness that typically characterized vegetarian cookbooks. Her approach proved that meatless dishes

could be flavorful, complex, and of endless variety. But that was not all. "In these strange 1970s, ominous and new dramatic reasons are compelling more people to reexamine their eating habits," she wrote. Chemical additives, pesticides, and animal cruelty all troubled her, but so did the "standard American diet . . . so appalling in its lack of imagination." Thomas challenged readers to break free of traditional meal courses and to experiment, as she herself "was just making things up." Her this-sounds-fun recipes even anticipated the crêpe and cheese fondue crazes. Renowned movie critic Roger Ebert not only praised Thomas's Oscar-nominated screenplay for *El Norte* (1984) but also gave her cookbook two thumbs up.

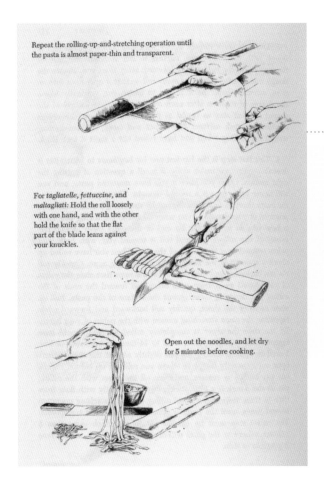

Repeat the rolling-up-and-stretching operation until the pasta is almost paper-thin and transparent.

For *tagliatelle, fettuccine,* and *maltagliati:* Hold the roll loosely with one hand, and with the other hold the knife so that the flat part of the blade leans against your knuckles.

Open out the noodles, and let dry for 5 minutes before cooking.

The Classic Italian Cook Book:
The Art of Italian Cooking and the Italian Art of Eating

 Marcella Hazan (1924–2013); Drawings by George Koizumi

 New York: Harper's Magazine Press

 1973

 General Collections

Spaghetti. Lasagna. Ravioli. Americans were already familiar with classic—but not necessarily authentically prepared—Italian dishes when Marcella Polini Hazan introduced her new countrymen to genuine Italian cooking. Her philosophy: flavor is everything and simplicity almost as much. A native of Cesenatico, Italy, she wrote this, her first cookbook, on request, inadvertently becoming the most influential and authoritative American author on Italian food. "The first useful thing to know about Italian cooking is that, as such, it actually doesn't exist," she explained, since Italian cuisine is *regional* cuisine, and her region was Emilia-Romagna, between Tuscany and the Adriatic Sea, where the vegetables "may well be the tastiest in the world." With instructional line drawings and the assurance that "there is not a single dish in this book that is beyond the competence of any moderately alert person," she provided more than 250 recipes. Her best known is for a buttery tomato sauce that has remained steadfastly popular. "In Italy the source of the very best Italian food is the home kitchen," she declared. "There is no reason why this should not be equally true here."

Julie Eisenhower's Cookbook for Children

 Julie Nixon Eisenhower (b. 1948)

 New York: Doubleday. Cover © SEPS licensed by Curtis Licensing, Indianapolis. All rights reserved.

 1975

General Collections

The daughter of President Richard Nixon and the wife of President Dwight Eisenhower's grandson, Julie Nixon Eisenhower curated this collection of simple recipes to introduce the basics of cooking to children. All recipes require fifteen minutes or fewer to prepare. She included recipes from her "famous friends," including Mister Rogers's Snow Pudding, Honey Bananas ("a favorite from Big Bird's kitchen"), and Frank Sinatra's Queen Cakes.

Bicentennial Heritage Recipes '76

 Beta Sigma Phi International

 Montgomery, AL: Favorite Recipes Press

 1976

General Collections

A red-white-and-blue descendant of community cookbooks, this compilation was issued during the US Bicentennial as the commemoration and celebration of American heritage paired especially well with marketing and fundraising. Produced by Beta Sigma Phi, an international, non-collegiate-based sorority, this collection of "old-fashioned, newly refined recipes" includes colonial-era and nineteenth-century historical tidbits, such as making a "pye with pippins" from 1683. The variety in American cuisine and its influences is reflected in the names of many dishes, such as Beef Curry in a Hurry with Cheese-Corn Bread Topper; Bayou Chico Shrimp Dip; and Cherokee Meat Loaf. An old Pennsylvania Dutch dessert, Shoofly Pie, earned its name from the cook having to wave off pests drawn to "this sweet, sticky confection." Many recipe names are attributed to relatives, with Grandma cited three times more often than Mom.

TO SERVE MAN: *a cookbook for people*

by Karl Würf
illustrated by Jack Bozzi
foreword by Margaret St. Clair

Owlswick Press
Philadelphia
1976

TO SERVE MAN

MAN-LOAF

Once basic Meat-Loaf has been mastered, this recipe becomes the starting point for an almost infinite set of variations. Of the standard ways to use ground Man—which also include Chili and Sausage, covered elsewhere in this work, and Manburger, which is too well-known to require special instructions—Man-Loaf, because of this flexibility, is best adapted to the problem of a fortnight or so of leftovers.

—Meat—
3 pounds ground Man
—Eggs—
2 eggs, lightly beaten
—Something dry—
1 cup cracker, toast, or bread crumbs; or quick-cooking barley; or 1/2 cup rice, pre-soaked 1 hour in 1 cup of water; or grated potato
—Seasonings—
2 tsp. salt, to taste
1/2 tsp. pepper, to taste
Perhaps 2 tsp. chopped onion or chives
Maybe 1 green pepper, chopped
If desired, 2 to 4 tsp. catsup
Or 4 tsp. Worcestershire sauce
Or even 1/2 tsp. sage, basil, or ground ginger
—And extra liquid—
1 to 2 cups milk, soup stock, tomato juice, or water

[24]

To Serve Man: *A Cookbook for People*

 Karl Würf (1929–2010)

 Philadelphia: Owlswick Press

 1976

Situated in the tradition of offbeat cookbooks, this one takes its title literally: it is a cookbook with "recipes" for serving humans. Karl Würf—a pseudonym for George Scithers—was inspired by a 1950 short story with the same title by fellow science fiction writer Damon Knight. The surprise ending reveals that a book, *To Serve Man*, created by seemingly amiable aliens, is not about aiding humanity, but *eating* it. In 1962, the short story was adapted on *The Twilight Zone*, in an episode considered one of the show's best. The line revealing the twist, "It's a cookbook!" has been spoofed by *The Simpsons* in a 1990 episode, and by the films *The Naked Gun 2 ½* (1991) and *Madagascar* (2005). The recipes include Texas Chili with Cowboy, Mannerschnitzel, Minceman Pie, Person Stroganoff, and the pictured Man Loaf.

The Key to Chinese Cooking

 Irene Kuo (1919–1993)

 New York: Knopf

 1977

 General Collections

Regarded as a masterpiece of Chinese cuisine in America, *The Key to Chinese Cooking* was written by Irene Kuo, a native of China who became the proprietor of two successful restaurants in New York City. Kuo appeared on talk shows hosted by Johnny Carson, Joan Rivers, and David Frost, attracting the attention of legendary cookbook editor Judith Jones in the mid-1970s. Illustrated with beautiful calligraphic scrolls created by Kuo's husband, the first section focuses on Chinese techniques, styles, and equipment; the second includes recipes. An appendix lists traditional Chinese ingredients with instructions for where to find them.

THE
KEY TO
CHINESE
COOKING

IRENE KUO

DRAWINGS BY CAROLYN MOY

CALLIGRAPHIC SEALS DESIGNED BY C. C. KUO

Alfred · A · Knopf / New York

19 77

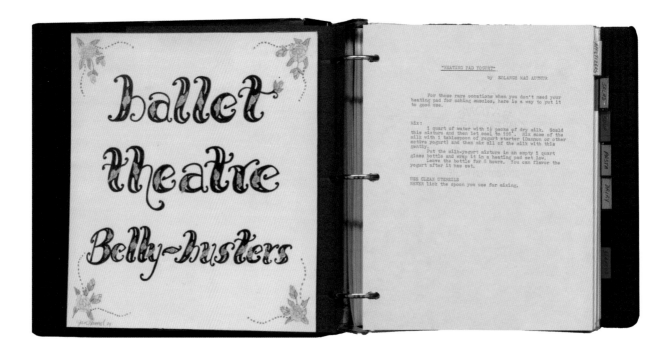

 ABT Dancers

 1979

 American Ballet Theatre Archive, Music Division

Ballet Theatre Belly-Busters Cookbook

In 1979, the corps de ballet of the American Ballet Theatre went on strike over low wages, causing the first labor stoppage in the troupe's history. To raise funds, the strikers held a benefit auction and performance, where they auctioned off this cookbook, made up of recipes submitted by the dancers. The winning bid of fifty dollars was only ten dollars less than a tutu belonging to ballerina Gelsey Kirkland. Several recipes have tongue-in-cheek connections to the dancers' craft; for example, ballerina Francia Kovak submitted a recipe for Nutcracker Sweet, a Russian teacake referencing Tchaikovsky's famous ballet. Another contributor, Solange MacArthur, included a recipe for Heating Pad Yogurt, which instructed dancers to make yogurt via their heating pads "for those rare occasions when you don't need your heating pad for aching muscles." In 2016, the Library of Congress acquired the only copy of the cookbook, as part of its American Ballet Theatre archives.

"More Time for Lovin'"

I've got
more
time for lovin
since I got my
Microwave
Oven

Cookbook
Common Sense Microwave
by Donovan Jon Fandre

I've Got "More Time for Lovin'" Since I Got My Microwave Oven

 Donovan Jon Fandre (b. 1935)

 Oakland: Friedmans Microwave Ovens

 1979

General Collections

The author's apron says it all. As new technology, busier schedules, and more women entering the work force reshaped cooking and dining in the 1970s, millions of Americans cleared space on their kitchen counters for a new appliance—the revolutionary warp-speed microwave oven. A baked potato that once needed an hour in a standard oven could now be zapped (or "nuked") and ready in about seven minutes. Donovan Jon Fandre, who provided both his favorite recipes and seasoned advice on supercharged cooking techniques, observed that "If you enjoy cooking and use common sense, you'll love your microwave oven. But if you're a lousy cook, the microwave will only make you a faster lousy cook." Fandre's book appeared as microwave ovens were catching on: in 1978, only 12 percent of American homes had one, but by 1997, more than 90 percent of households apparently had more time for romance.

The Wonderful Wizard of Oz Cook Book

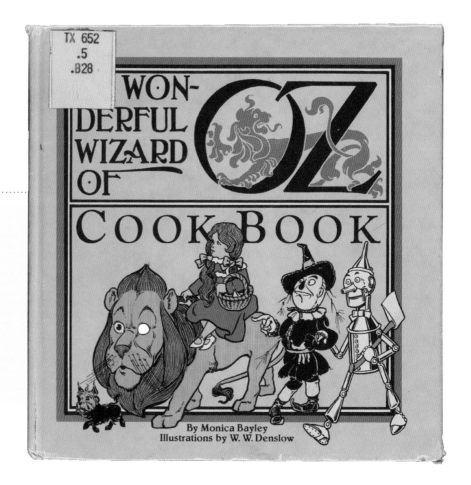

 Monica Bayley

 New York: Macmillan

 1981

 General Collections

Since at least the 1960s, cookbooks have taken inspiration from famous novels, characters, and authors, such as *Little House on the Prairie*, *A Confederacy of Dunces*, Winnie-the-Pooh, Harry Potter, Sherlock Holmes, Emily Dickinson, and H. P. Lovecraft. Monica Bayley chose the 1900 first edition of *The Wonderful Wizard of Oz* by L. Frank Baum for this homage. She included food items from Baum's text, for example pairing porridge with an excerpt that refers to Dorothy having a bowl of it. Some dishes are her own creations, such as Cowardly Lion Quivering Gelatin. The book is organized by location in Oz, leading to colorful ingredients that line up with the book's vibrant geography; hence a recipe for corn bread in the Yellow Brick Road section and Royal Green Beans in the Emerald City chapter.

Sushi

 Mia Detrick (b. 1945)

 San Francisco: Chronicle Books

 1981

 General Collections

Although sushi bars drew devotees in 1960s Los Angeles, most Americans then had never tasted the Japanese delicacy—or even heard of it. That all changed in the 1980s, as an increase in Asian immigration led to a surge in sushi bars and a more fully developed appreciation across the country for rice and raw seafood artfully seasoned, garnished, and presented. Unable to find a sushi book in English, Mia Detrick traveled up and down the West Coast sampling sushi bars and interviewing chefs, then wrote one herself. "Sushi is the aristocrat of snack food and worthy of being a meal in itself," she explains in the first work in English solely dedicated to the subject. Detrick introduces sushi's origins, history, and variety; offers illustrated instructions for making sushi at home; and describes the arduous chef apprenticeship, meticulous preparation, and traditional etiquette that give sushi its standing as high art. Kathryn Kleinman's accompanying fine-arts gallery of photographs seconds the notion.

Entertaining

Martha Stewart (b. 1941), text with Elizabeth Hawes (b. 1940)

New York: C. N. Potter

1981

General Collections

Queen Victoria, Coco Chanel, and Jackie Kennedy Onassis imparted outsize influence on popular taste and the ideal lifestyle, but only Martha Stewart packaged it all—the kitchen arts, design, decorating, gardening, crafts, entertaining, fashion, and beautiful living—and did it through all forms of media. As America's first lifestyle mogul (and first American woman to become a self-made billionaire), she was the precursor to the lifestyle gurus and social influencers that emerged online in the early 2000s. *Entertaining*, the inaugural edition of Stewart's nearly one hundred books over the next forty years, sold the idea of a considered and curated domestic lifestyle as a pleasurable pursuit and potential full-time occupation, of which gracious entertaining was a key element. A *New York Times* review called it "beautiful" but declared that "one would no more dream of cooking from Mrs. Stewart's . . . book, spattering it with olive oil as you work, than would think of thumbing through an expensive art book while eating fried chicken." Instead, it was meant for browsing and inspiration. Stewart provided guidance, menus, and recipes that to the general reader were both manageable (Sunday Omelette Brunch for Eight to Ten) and implausible (A Catered Wedding Luncheon for Two Hundred Seventy).

Chez Panisse Menu Cookbook

 Alice Waters (b. 1944)

 New York: Random House

 1982

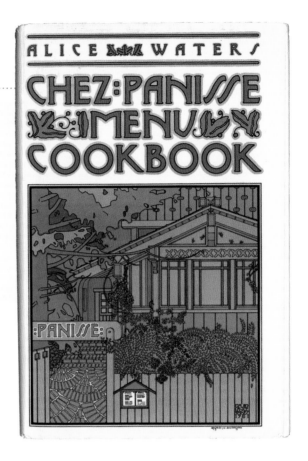 General Collections

Farm-to-table champion, Francophile, and California cuisine godmother Alice Waters stirred up American gastronomy like batter for her buckwheat crêpes. Her Berkeley-based rustic restaurant, Chez Panisse, established in 1971, instantly developed a cult-like following for its novel insistence on serving local, seasonal, high-quality fresh food in an era that expected inexpensive, year-round produce. This method was the antithesis of agribusiness and the inspiration for modern farmers markets nationwide. In her daily excursions to meet food growers and artisans, Waters changed the existing dynamic from business as usual to one of collaboration. For Waters, "my definition of fresh is that the perfect little lettuces are carefully hand-picked from the hillside garden and served within a few hours." And when the desired ingredient isn't at its best, "find one that is, and go from there." That methodology often meant devising recipes that went unrecorded when she and her chefs were too busy improvising a dish to take notes. Over time Waters and her staff got better at "writing down recipes that really click," leading to a series of cookbooks. The first, *Chez Panisse Menu Cookbook*, chronicled the early years of one the most influential restaurants in American history and included recipes that showed an affection for its trademark ingredient: baked, crumbled, marinated, or melted goat cheese.

"This Could Undermine the Entire Foundation of American Business"

Herblock [Herbert Lawrence Block] (1909–2001)

Drawing

1984

Prints and Photographs Division

As Congress considered eliminating tax-deductible business expenses, editorial cartoonist Herblock of the *Washington Post* pointed out the likely corporate response. Thirty years earlier, the *Atlanta Constitution* had observed that the classic three-martini lunch was "enjoyed by the comfortably retired, the indispensable man, and those with generous expense accounts." Those accounts grew ever more generous during the postwar era, and such a lunch reached its apex as a sign of professional success and occupational indulgence in the 1950s and 1960s. It gradually dribbled out of fashion amid changing lifestyles, corporate belt-tightening, and the Tax Reform Act of 1986, as those with company credit cards increasingly opted for iced tea or a Diet Coke.

Wine Cooler

Chimney Glass   11 oz.
½ fill Glass with Ice
3 oz. White or Red Wine
½ oz. Orange Juice
Fill to top with Lemon-Lime
   Soda or Soda.
Squeeze wedge of Lime.

Garnish with cherry and
orange slice on a pick.

247

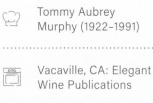

Tommy Aubrey
Murphy (1922–1991)

Vacaville, CA: Elegant
Wine Publications

1984

General Collections

Elegant Wine Cocktails: *The Complete Wine Cocktail Guide*

Wine is fermented and not distilled, thus it nominally does not fit the classic definition of a cocktail ingredient. However, as this pocket-sized guide argues, wine is "the long-reigning host and subtle catalyst to a gamut of occasions." Many of the book's 111 wine-based concoctions resemble, in appearances and ingredients, their hard liquor counterparts. The Salty Dog, for example, combines Chablis, ice, and grapefruit juice in a double rock glass with a salted rim. Others, such as the Banana Ginger Supreme and the Pina Frio, are singular inventions, incorporating ingredients such as a whole banana or a hollowed-out pineapple. Born and raised on a Cherokee reservation in Tennessee, Tommy Murphy developed an affinity for wine through world travel. He also wrote *American Standard 100+ Bartender's Handbook: The Complete Bar Guide*, *Classic Cocktails*, and *Tropical Cocktails*.

Mixology
in the Movies

THE ART OF MIXOLOGY DOESN'T GET AS MUCH SCREEN TIME AS BARROOM BRAWLS, DRUNKEN SOLILOQUIES, SLAPSTICK INTOXICATION, AND ALCOHOL-FUELED PLOTS, BUT IT HAS INTRODUCED SOME MEMORABLE CHARACTERS IN FILM HISTORY. IN THE SCREWBALL COMEDY *THE THIN MAN* (1934), DETECTIVE NICK CHARLES (WILLIAM POWELL) DEMONSTRATES THE NUANCES OF USING A COCKTAIL SHAKER. "THE IMPORTANT THING IS THE RHYTHM," NICK ADVISES HIS AUDIENCE OF BARTENDERS, EXECUTING A FEW DANCE STEPS AS HE MIXES HIS DRINK. "ALWAYS HAVE RHYTHM IN YOUR SHAKING. NOW A MANHATTAN YOU SHAKE TO FOX-TROT TIME, A BRONX TO TWO-STEP TIME, A DRY MARTINI YOU ALWAYS SHAKE TO WALTZ TIME."

The Coen brothers revived interest in the White Russian cocktail, which dates back to 1949 and features prominently in their 1998 film *The Big Lebowski*. With just three ingredients—vodka, coffee liqueur, and cream over ice—even the stoner known as the Dude (Jeff Bridges) can remember the recipe, although in a pinch he is seen to use a non-dairy powdered creamer. Similarly, the modern Cosmopolitan cocktail, developed in the 1980s, was popularized by the television series *Sex and the City* (1998) as the hip drink of choice for best friends Carrie, Miranda, Charlotte, and Samantha. In season two, episode seven, Samantha says to a bartender, "Another Cosmopolitan, please," naming the neon pink drink that practically became another character in the show. Its legacy was referenced in the feature film released in 2008: "Why did we ever stop drinking these?" asks Miranda. "Because everyone else started," says Carrie, which was pretty much what actually happened.

The most famous and longest running drink order belongs to the James Bond film franchise, although 007 doesn't mention it first. In *Dr. No* (1962), a steward delivering his drink tells Bond (Sean Connery), "one medium dry vodka Martini. Mixed like you said, sir. And not stirred." It's not until the third film, *Goldfinger* (1964), that Bond utters one of the most iconic lines in movie history, asking for "a Martini, shaken, not stirred."

Throughout the series, other actors playing Bond, his associates, and his enemies also utter the line. There has long been speculation, though, why a man so worldly and familiar with liquor would not want his drink stirred, which is the usual recommendation for mixing Martinis. A common explanation is that shaken ice dilutes the alcohol, reducing its potency, thus Bond remains clearheaded while conducting serious spy business.

The 2006 film *Casino Royale*, starring Daniel Craig in his first outing as Bond, found the secret agent ordering a dry Martini with his most explicit directions yet: "three measures of Gordon's, one of vodka, half a measure of Kina Lillet, shake it over ice, then add a thin slice of lemon peel." Later, an unusually stressed Bond again orders his signature drink and the bartender confirms that it should be "shaken, not stirred?" More than forty years of movie certitude is turned on its head when a perturbed Bond responds, "Do I look like I give a damn?"

Tom Cruise (pictured) stars as Brian Flanagan, an ambitious would-be entrepreneur who, with the help of a seasoned pro (Bryan Brown) becomes the best bartender on Manhattan's Upper East Side. But when he meets Jordan Mooney (Elisabeth Shue), an independent artist, their spirited romance brings a new perspective to the cocksure bartender's life in "Cocktail," a new romantic drama from director Roger Donaldson ("No Way Out"). A Touchstone Pictures presentation in association with Silver Screen Partners III, "Cocktail" is produced by Ted Field and Robert W. Cort from a screenplay by Heywood Gould, based on Gould's book of the same name. Buena Vista distributes.
CTBB-2
photo: RICHARD CORMAN
Permission is hereby granted to newspapers and magazines to reproduce this picture on the condition that it is accompanied by "© MCMLXXXVIII Touchstone Pictures. All Rights Reserved".

Cocktail

© 1988 Touchstone Pictures. Publicity still. Photo: Richard Corman. Motion Picture, Broadcasting, and Recorded Sound Division.

Modern-day heirs to saloon keeper and showman Jerry Thomas, "flair bartenders" execute bottle flips, spins, stalls, ice tossing, the multi-pour, the shadow pass (throwing and catching a bottle behind one's back), and dozens of other moves—all while properly making a drink quickly. Los Angeles bartender John Bandy taught actors Tom Cruise and Bryan Brown tricks for the movie *Cocktail*, and its box office success further spread the art of flair bartending. The film also popularized its signature drink, the Red Eye, which veteran bartender Doug Coughlin (Brown) uses as a cure for hangovers—mostly his own. Various recipes exist, but all use tomato juice, beer, and a raw egg, unstirred. Doug's version also includes tabasco sauce and two aspirin; an ounce of vodka and a dash of pepper are other common ingredients.

Mister Roberts

1955. Lobby card, Warner Bros. Motion Picture, Broadcasting, and Recorded Sound Division.

In a classic scene, officers aboard the *USS Reluctant*, a supply vessel operating in the backwaters of the Pacific during World War II, develop an iconic recipe for scotch. Doc (William Powell), left, using medical grain alcohol, added other ingredients found nearby: Coca-Cola for color, "one drop of iodine—for taste," and "one drop of hair tonic for age. That'll age the daylights out of it." After a skeptical Mr. Roberts (Henry Fonda), center, chokes down a sip, he agrees that it does "taste a little like scotch," to the delight of hapless laundry and morale officer Ensign Pulver (Jack Lemmon, in an Oscar-winning performance). Until the 1970s, lobby cards were regularly displayed in theaters to promote upcoming and current films; unlike the larger movie posters, these cards featured photo stills from notable scenes.

My Little Chickadee

1940. Film still, Universal Pictures. Motion Picture, Broadcasting, and Recorded Sound Division.

In this comedy western that also starred Mae West, W. C. Fields, center, played conman Cuthbert J. Twillie. Fields—whose movie characters were usually well-dressed curmudgeons with a fondness for drink—demonstrated his genius for both verbal and physical comedy as a temporary bartender behind a ridiculously long bar and as a cardsharp. In the poker game scene shown here, he casually tells the other players that "During one of our treks through Afghanistan—we lost our corkscrew—compelled to live on food and water—for several days."

SALADE OLIVIER, GEORGE BALANCHINE

8–12 SERVINGS

1   cucumber, peeled
1   dill pickle (German style; that is, pickled without
       garlic)
    The meat of 1 3-pound roast chicken (or roast
       pheasant), cubed
4   boiled potatoes, peeled and sliced
1   cup cooked peas, well drained
¾   cup mayonnaise
½   cup sour cream
4   teaspoons Dijon mustard
    Salt and freshly ground pepper to taste
4   hard-boiled eggs, quartered
2   tablespoons capers, drained
24 black and green olives, pitted and halved
4   ripe tomatoes, quartered

Slice the cucumber and the pickle in quarters lengthwise, then in thin slices crosswise. Mix them with the chicken, potatoes, and peas. Mix the mayonnaise, sour cream, and mustard together. Add to the salad and toss well. Season with salt and pepper. Garnish with the eggs, capers, olives, and tomatoes.

The Gold and Fizdale Cookbook

 Arthur Gold (1917–1990) and Robert Fizdale (1920–1995)

 New York: Random House

 1984

 General Collections

For decades, the piano duo and romantic couple Arthur Gold and Robert Fizdale were mainstays of the classical music scene, championing works by contemporary composers like John Cage, Francis Poulenc, and Samuel Barber. In the 1970s, when Gold began experiencing pain in his hands, the couple turned from performance to writing. They dedicated *The Gold and Fizdale Cookbook* to their friend, choreographer George Balanchine, and included this recipe of his favorite dish, Olivier Salad. Created by Belgian-French chef Lucien Olivier—who served Czar Nicolas II in the late nineteenth century—it is more commonly known as Russian salad.

The Hispanic Cookbook/La Cocina Hispano-Americana:
Traditional and Modern Recipes in English and Spanish

 Nilda Luz Rexach (b. 1929)

 Secaucus, NJ: Carol Publishing Group

 1995; first published 1985 by L. Stuart as *The Hispanic-American Cookbook*

 General Collections

In one of the earliest cookbooks in the United States to feature Latin American cuisine in both English and Spanish, Nilda Luz Rexach shared her collection of basic, "easy to prepare" recipes. A New York City schoolteacher from Santurce, Puerto Rico, Rexach had a regular food column in *El Vigilante* before developing her cookbook, the first edition of which appeared in 1985. Her timing was spot on, as previously hard-to-find items, such as sofrito, plantains, and yuccas, had become more widely available in American supermarkets. Although many recipes draw from her Puerto Rican background, others show newer influences: she offers recipes for both traditional Tembleque, a coconut and cinnamon dessert pudding, and Tembleque New York Style, using packaged ingredients. Her recipe for paella is extraordinary, with its combination of a half-dozen vegetables, chicken, sausage, lobster, shrimp, octopus, and clams.

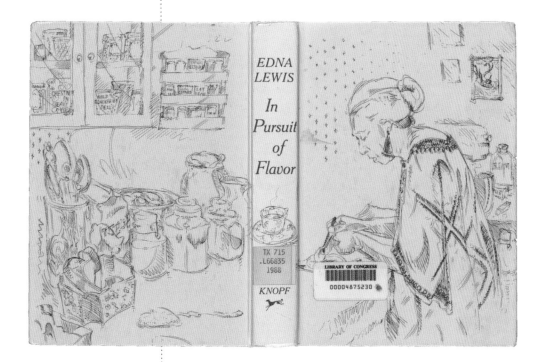

In Pursuit of Flavor

 Edna Lewis (1916–2006) with Mary Goodbody (b. 1949)

 New York: Knopf

 1988

 General Collections

A highly decorated chef, Edna Lewis grew up in Freetown, Virginia, a hamlet her emancipated grandfather and others founded shortly after the Civil War. "In those days, we lived by the seasons, and I quickly discovered that food tastes best when it is naturally ripe and ready to eat," she wrote, before leading the reader to the garden, orchard, farmyard, rivers, and the ocean. As a New York City chef in the early 1950s, she impressed members of the bohemian arts scene and Southern expats Truman Capote and William Faulkner, who found a welcome taste of home at her East Fifty-Seventh Street establishment. Lewis's earlier cookbook, *The Taste of Country Cooking* (1976), catapulted her to icon status as she reclaimed for black cooks their historical place at the forefront of refined Southern cuisine. *In Pursuit of Flavor* was her magnum opus, with two hundred recipes, accumulated wisdom, and illustrations of her at her craft. "As a child . . . I thought all food tasted delicious. After growing up, I didn't think food tasted the same," she observes. "So it has been my lifelong effort to try and recapture those good flavors of the past."

The Dooky Chase Cookbook

 Leah Chase (1923–2019)

 New Orleans: Pelican Publishing.
Used with permission of Pelican
Publishing. All rights reserved

 1990

 General Collections

CREOLE JAMBALAYA

1 lb. smoked ham (cubed)
½ lb. chaurice (hot
   sausage cut in pieces)
½ lb. smoked sausage
   (cut in ½-inch slices)
1 cup chopped onions
3 cups uncooked rice
¼ cup chopped green
   onions
½ tsp. paprika
1 tbsp. chopped parsley
1 tsp. ground thyme
1 tsp. chopped garlic
½ cup chopped green
   pepper
1 tsp. salt
1 bay leaf
1 lb. shrimp (peeled and
   deveined)
4 cups boiling water

Place ham, sausages, and onions in 3-quart saucepan. Cover and cook over medium heat until onions are soft. No need to add any oil as the meat will provide enough fat for cooking. Add rice and stir well. Add all other ingredients. Bring to a boil. Let boil for 5 minutes. Lower heat. Cover pot tightly and let cook slowly for 35 minutes or until rice is tender. With a fork, fluff rice up, mixing sausages well. Yield: 6 to 8 servings.

100 • THE DOOKY CHASE COOKBOOK

Dooky Chase's Restaurant, located in the Tremé neighborhood of New Orleans, has been serving customers since 1941. Leah Chase married Edward "Dooky" Chase Jr. in 1946 and helped turn his father's sandwich shop into one of the most famous creole restaurants in the country, showcasing southern recipes like this one for jambalaya. Besides offering food, the restaurant operated as a hub during the Civil Rights Movement, even cashing checks for African Americans whom local banks discriminated against. Chase served her dishes to Freedom Riders, Thurgood Marshall, Martin Luther King Jr., and Barack Obama, who made the mistake of trying to add tabasco sauce to her gumbo. In a 2018 interview with the Library of Congress's American Folklife Center, she recounted swatting the hot sauce packet away, telling the president, "You don't put hot stuff in my gumbo."

Tamalada (Making Tamales)

Fixing handmade tamales is a labor-intensive process that lends itself to a family or communal activity, thus the dish is often associated with festivals and holidays, especially Christmas. Tamale dough and fillings vary throughout Latin America and are rooted in Mesoamerican culture dating back thousands of years.

Carmen Lomas Garza (b. 1948)

Lithograph

1990

Prints and Photographs Division

The Black Family Reunion Cookbook:
Recipes and Food Memories

 National Council of Negro Women

 Memphis: Tradery House

 1991

 General Collections

When civil rights leader Mary McLeod Bethune, the daughter of a formerly enslaved couple, needed to raise funds for the girls' school she established—which later became Bethune-Cookman University—out came her money-making recipe for sweet potato pie. She later founded the National Council of Negro Women (NCNW) in 1935, and that organization, under the leadership of Dr. Dorothy Height, began the annual National Black Family Reunion in 1989. This cookbook, edited by longtime *Los Angeles Sentinel* food editor Libby Clark, was a natural offshoot from the summer celebration, bringing together favorite recipes, humorous recollections, and warm reminiscences of African-American foodways. Both well-known and known-only-to-their-family cooks contributed to the book, and the first of its 250 recipes is for Emancipation Proclamation Breakfast Cake (blueberry shortbread). Bethune's go-to pie recipe is featured as well, as are excerpts from her writings. Proceeds from the bestselling cookbook supported various NCNW initiatives around the country.

Fusion
Salads
for Any
Occasion

 Hugh Carpenter
(b. 1947) and Teri
Sandison (b. 1948)

 New York: Artisan

 1994

General Collections

Fusion Food Cookbook

Ancient civilizations naturally developed fusion cooking through conquest and the spice trade that wended its way from China, India, Arabia, and North Africa to the Mediterranean world and the far edges of Western Europe. That was thousands of years before Austrian chef Wolfgang Puck began serving dishes that mixed Asian, French, and California cuisine at Spago in 1982 on the Sunset Strip in Hollywood. It was there in California that the modern fusion cuisine movement originated and flourished, fueled by a diverse population, a plethora of specialty food shops, and a statewide penchant for innovation. Fusion is generally defined as the contrasting mix of various culinary traditions

and techniques, or as author Hugh Carpenter puts it, "cooking without boundaries." Carpenter, a chef and early cross-cultural enthusiast, and Teri Sandison, professional photographer, fused their own areas of expertise to produce the first fusion cookbook, a collection of 157 recipes that the couple spent five years testing and evaluating. Among the selections: Cajun Asian Ratatouille, Game Hens with Tamarind Glaze, and Szechwan Huevos Rancheros.

Joan Nathan (b. 1943)

 New York: Knopf

 1994

General Collections

Jewish Cooking in America

Self-described as "passionately interested in studying the roots of Jewish cuisine," Joan Nathan has dedicated her life to preserving, honoring, and sharing Jewish culinary traditions. Her time working for the mayor of Israel's capital city inspired her first cookbook, *The Flavor of Jerusalem* (1975). Her masterpiece, *Jewish Cooking in America*, won both the Julia Child Cookbook Award and a James Beard Award. Alongside foods associated with Eastern European Ashkenazi Jews, Nathan also modified recipes that are not normally kosher and included foods from Sephardic Jews, whose cuisine has Mediterranean and Levantine influences. Thus, recipes for gefilte fish, chicken livers, and kugel accompany instructions for preparing salmon

ceviche, jambalaya with veal sausage, and Turkish zucchini pie. Like Julia Child, she also produced and hosted a television show based on her work, *Jewish Cooking in America with Joan Nathan*, introducing Jewish cuisine to a larger audience. Her legacy of celebrating Jewish food prompted the *Jerusalem Post* to declare her the "Matriarch of Jewish Cooking," and in 2015, she joined the likes of Child, M. F. K. Fisher, Marcella Hazan, and Edna Lewis when the Les Dames d'Escoffier International granted her their Grand Dame Award.

Seagram's Bartending Guide

Founded in Ontario in 1857, Seagram's was one of the largest alcoholic beverage providers in the world when this bartending guide was published. Besides traditional cocktails, the book also featured food recipes that use spirits as ingredients. In addition to those shown here, for Calypso Grilled Shrimp with spiced rum and vegetable dip with anisette, there are instructions for soup made with Chardonnay; a Zucchini Martini with sautéed squash in gin and vermouth; Dijon lamb chops cooked in wine; and decadent desserts that call for Godiva liqueur.

Seagram's

New York: Viking

1995

General Collections

Fast Food: Cars and Cuisine

SINCE THE FIRST ROAD, ROAD FOOD HAS BEEN ESSENTIAL TO PEOPLE ON THE MOVE, WHETHER BETWEEN CAVES OR METROPOLISES. THE MODERN ROAD, THOUGH, COMES FULL CIRCLE WITH THESE TWO AUTOMOTIVELY INSPIRED WORKS.

When *The Motorist's Luncheon Book* was published in 1923, about 15 percent of Americans had cars, and most of those drivers were ferrying about family, friends, or employers. "The love of the great outdoors grows with each new automobile," observed May Southworth, as more day-trippers packed picnic baskets and drove off in search of ever more distant and scenic locales. She recommended using the "expensive refrigerator basket *de luxe*," if possible, and "a little sociable chafing dish," but also observed that "To be a true, comfortable disciple of the road one must acquire the habit of using thermos bottles." The book contains preparation and packing tips for each of the extraordinarily varied hot and cold menus, such as chop suey with rice, buttered rolls, pickled broccoli, hot Ceylon tea, and eclairs.

More than a half-century later, when the first edition of *Manifold Destiny* appeared in 1989, about 75 percent of Americans owned cars, though few were simultaneously driving while dinner cooked under the hood. The concept was not entirely new, but the effort to popularize it was. "The point is that you can make better meals for yourself, on your engine, than the vast majority of the roadside stands can make for you," wrote the authors. The key benefit of car-engine cooking is that "simmering foods in their own juices in a sealed package" of aluminum foil enhances the flavor using already available heat en route to your destination. Another advantage is that varying temperatures on different parts of the engine allow for quick or slow-cooking methods, depending on the entrees and side dishes. Unlike traditional modern recipes that give instructions for time and temperature settings, the directions here are given by the distance driven; plan on fifty-five miles for Cajun shrimp.

Manifold Destiny:

The One! The Only! Guide to Cooking on Your Car Engine

Chris Maynard (1948–2012) and Bill Scheller (b. 1949), New York: Villard Books, 1989. General Collections.

Chris Maynard and Bill Scheller

MANIFOLD DESTINY

"CAJUN" SHRIMP

On a recent trip through Louisiana we stopped to check out the shelves in a Pick and Pay supermarket in Lake Arthur. It was the first time we ever saw *gallon* jars of rendered pork fat in a butcher case. Next we browsed through the condiment and spice selections, and realized that a lot of what's been sweeping the country as "Cajun" cooking increasingly comes out of jars—jars of precooked roux, jars of spice mixes for meat and fish, jars with drawings of fat men on them. In short, what started out as a bona fide regional cuisine has become a premixed abomination designed to make fat people fatter. We don't know what the life expectancy is down there, but we do know that it's possible to travel through Cajun country for a week without encountering any food that isn't fried, with the exception of coffee and salad. Here's a sample, with the brand names deleted.

Distance: 55 miles

Rendered pork fat
1 pound shrimp from the supermarket
Assorted jars of whatever "Cajun" seasonings you've seen advertised

At home or on the road, heat fat until it liquefies. If you're a real diehard car cook, you might want to do this on an idling engine, using one of the cleaned-out tuna cans you keep on hand to make **Eggs in Purgatory** (page 68) in the Northeast. Peel shrimp and devein if they're large. Then dredge shrimp in fat and dust heavily with the powdered spices. Wrap in foil.

Place on a medium-hot part of the engine, and cook for about 1 hour. It doesn't matter if the shrimp are overcooked, since you're eating a concept, not a food.

96

BLACKENED ROADFISH

As in the previous recipe, think of the concept and not the food. What's important about this dish is driving along thinking, "I'm cooking blackened fish and you're not." It's the same idea as having a car that can go 150 MPH even if you never get it over 65.

Distance: 50 miles

1 pound firm white fish fillets, cut thin
Your choice of premixed "Cajun" spices

At home or on the road, cover fish on both sides with a heavy layer of spices, pressing them in with your hands. Place on foil spread with butter and wrap tightly.

Cook about 25 minutes per side.

The One! The Only! Guide to Cooking on Your Car Engine!

Manifold DESTINY

Chris Maynard and Bill Scheller

The MOTORIST'S LUNCHEON BOOK

For the motor picnicker or camper, this handy little cook-book will solve all questions about food.

Equipment necessary, supplies which have been proven practical, balanced menus, recipes—everything is given in the book to make delightful and delicious the meals of the amateur gypsy.

MAY E. SOUTHWORTH

HARPER & BROTHERS, PUBLISHERS
Established 1817

The Motorist's Luncheon Book

May E. Southworth, New York: Harper & Brothers, 1923. Katherine Golden Bitting Collection on Gastronomy, Rare Book and Special Collections Division.

El Taco Zamorano, Food Truck,
International Blvd. at High Street, Oakland

 Camilo José Vergara (b. 1944)

 Photograph

 March 10, 2020

 Prints and Photographs Division

CHAPTER 6

Something You've Never Had Before"

THE VARIETY OF THE AMERICAN FEAST

Cookbooks and cocktails in the twenty-first century continue to take the measure of the times, usually looking back and gazing ahead simultaneously. Cocktails connoisseur Robert Simonson observed that "If there is one trend that epitomizes the whole of the cocktail renaissance . . . it is fresh ingredients. During the '90s, the cocktail bar slowly converted itself from a supermarket aisle, filled with shelf-stable products rife with preservatives and chemicals, to a green grocer, where freshly plucked and sourced ingredients—juices, garnishes, eggs, everything—crowded the bar top every service." Similarly, the concept of fresh ingredients received a fresh look through the modern eco-conscious farm-to-table movement, "flexitarian" diets featuring plant-based foods, and urban farmers' markets.

The forecasted demise of the traditional printed cookbook has not yet come to pass; if anything, it is as robust and alive as ever. In the United States, more than 20 million new cookbooks are sold annually, not to mention heavy sales traffic in used copies. When personal computers came on the market in the 1980s, a big selling point was that a purchaser could use it to organize and automatically sort all their recipes. It was later thought that the cornucopia of recipes shared and archived online would replace the splattered, penciled in, and sticky-noted cookbook by the stove. Surely, recipe ebooks, easily updatable and searchable, interactive, and all on one device, would do in the old static cookbook. But no.

The cookbook, whatever its form, remains essential, and peculiarly versatile. The kitchen cookbook, to work from; the coffee table cookbook, to admire and peruse; and the couch cookbook, to read for pleasure, may be one and the same, or not. Yet each contains centuries of accumulated wisdom and innovation that have made possible the dishes and meals we each have come to regard as American feasts.

The Easy-Bake Oven Gourmet

 David Hoffman (b. 1953)

 Philadelphia: Running Press

 2003

 General Collections

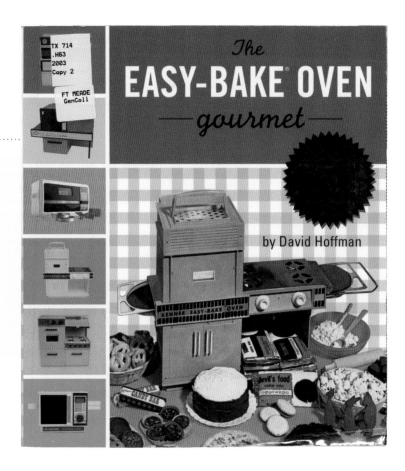

The Easy-Bake Oven has been to millions of girls—and some of their brothers—what an equally coveted Michelin star is to restaurants. Introduced in 1963, the toy kitchen appliance came with utensils, powdered mixes, and a recipe booklet for baking three-and-a-half-inch-wide cookies and cakes under a pair of 100-watt light bulbs. Author David Hoffman notes that with what seemed like endless cooking times of six to sixteen minutes, "half-cooked chocolate cakes [became] a dietary staple of middle-class families everywhere." He also reports that many leading chefs began their training as Easy-Bakers fixing brownies and gingerbread. This cookbook, released on the occasion of the little oven's fortieth anniversary, features one-serving gourmet recipes, such as Rob Feenie's Roasted Quail Breast with Wild Mushrooms and Pomme Anna, Erik Blauberg's Deep Dish Truffle Lobster Pie, and Emily Luchetti's Pear Streusel Coffee Cake. At last there was an Easy-Bake Oven cookbook accommodating the higher end of ages "eight and up."

New Junior Cook Book

 Better Homes and Gardens

 Des Moines: Meredith Books, seventh edition

 2004

 General Collections

A kid's preferred grocery list might be heavy on mac and cheese, tater tots, and pizza, but this vibrantly illustrated cookbook for young chefs also touches on salads, fruit cups, and dressings to cover veggies so "you'll never know they're there." Spiral bound and wrapped in Better Homes and Gardens' traditional red and white checkered tablecloth motif, this high-energy seventh iteration covers the basics in culinary lingo, cooking tools, and table manners. Early on the authors offer what is perhaps the most important advice a novice in the kitchen can receive: "Before you begin, read the recipe from start to finish." The first Better Homes and Gardens *Junior Cook Book* ("for the hostess and host of tomorrow"), published in 1955, featured hot dogs on the cover; in this edition there are no frankfurters but rather roast beef wraps, fajitas, and chicken stir-fry.

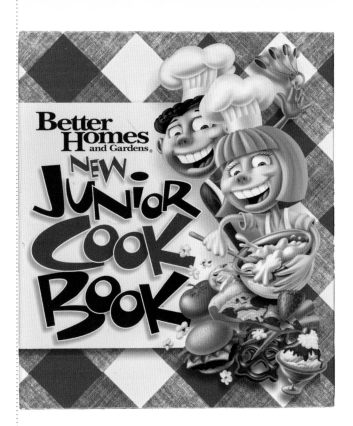

IndeBleu
Cocktail Menu

Washington, DC:
IndeBleu, map

2004

Geography & Map Division

The Washington, DC, restaurant and bar IndeBleu created its own version of the city's famous Metro map to highlight their various cocktails on offer. Drinkers could choose from the champagne cocktails line, the Martini line, or even a shot line, with specific mixology creations taking the place of station names.

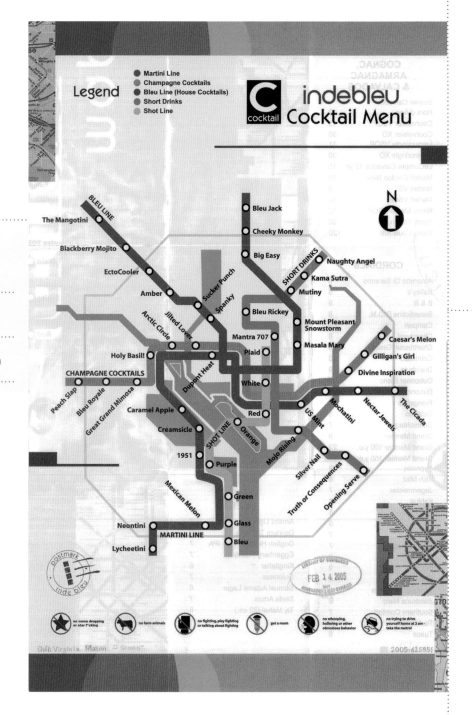

The New York City Sub-Culinary Map

Maira Kalman (b. 1949) and
Rick Meyerowitz (b. 1943)

Color photomechanical print

2004

Prints and Photographs Division

The idea for this altered New York City subway map came to artist Rick Meyerowitz while riding the subway and thinking about lunch. Meyerowitz and his collaborator, Maira Kalman, spent the next several months eating across the five boroughs and coming up with 650 new food-related names for stations and geographic landmarks, such as Yankee Pot Roast and Chalupas Field (replacing Yankee Stadium and the Mets' Citi Field), Upper Smoked Fish (Upper West Side), and Green Goddess (Liberty Island). Other names reveal the local ethnic cuisines on offer, such as three

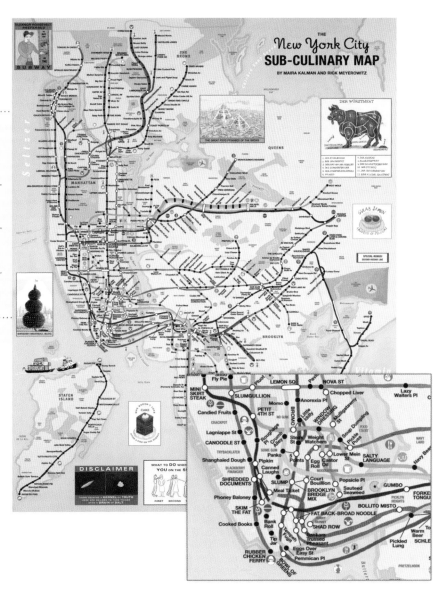

consecutive stations in the predominantly Hispanic neighborhood of Jackson Heights renamed to "Empanadas Av," "Chimichangas St" and "Tres Cervezas." After a year of research, drawing, and refining, the transformed map was published in the *New Yorker* in 2004.

500 Vegan Recipes:

An Amazing Variety of Delicious Recipes, from Chilis and Casseroles to Crumbles, Crisps, and Cookies

 Celine Steen and Joni-Marie Newman (b. 1975)

 Beverly, MA: Fair Winds Press

 2009

 General Collections

American vegan cookbooks date back to Russell Thacher Trall's *The Hygeian Home Cook-Book; or, Healthful and Palatable Food without Condiments*, published in 1874. But veganism did not draw mainstream attention in the United States for more than a century. Although less than five percent of Americans consider themselves full-time vegetarians (and far fewer as vegans), the hundreds of vegan titles published since 2000 reflect growing interest in plant-based meals. With a shorter list of acceptable ingredients, vegan recipes might seem as if they sprout from rather petite cookbooks.

This substantial volume proves otherwise. A bible for committed vegans, it also caters to omnivores wanting alternative meal options on hand. It might surprise meat-eaters that among the book's five hundred recipes the authors offer dishes such as Beefy Bacon Burger (no beef or bacon, but textured vegetable protein granules and imitation bacon bits), Seitan Chorizo Crumbles, and Shepherd's Pie with walnuts, lentils, and zucchini.

Tailgating
Tradition

AMERICA'S TAILGATING HERITAGE INCLUDES CONESTOGA WAGONS, CATTLE DRIVERS' CHUCK WAGONS, AND FOOD WAGONS THAT PROVISIONED EARLY COLLEGE FOOTBALL FANS. THEN CAME THE REAL BREAKTHROUGH: THE STATION WAGON, A FAMILY CAR THAT PEAKED IN POPULARITY FROM THE 1950S THROUGH THE 1970S. ITS LOWERED TAILGATE COULD FUNCTION AS A BUFFET OR PICNIC TABLE, TAKING CAR-SIDE GAME-DAY DINING TO NEW PLACES—SUCH AS CROWDED PARKING LOTS. "IF YOU THINK ABOUT IT, A PARKING LOT ISN'T HIGH ON THE LIST OF FUN PLACES TO STAND IN FIFTEEN-DEGREE WEATHER," WROTE HALL OF FAME NFL COACH AND BROADCASTER JOHN MADDEN IN HIS BOOK *ULTIMATE TAILGATING* (1998). "BUT SOMEHOW TAILGATING WITH YOUR FRIENDS AND FAMILY MAKES EVEN A PARKING LOT A GREAT PLACE TO HANG OUT. ANYTHING THAT CAN DO THAT TO A COUPLE OF ACRES OF ASPHALT HAS A LOT GOING FOR IT."

With the possible exception of hot dogs at the ballpark, underwhelming and overpriced stadium food made tailgating an especially attractive pre-game option. By the 1960s, come autumn, newspaper food sections and women's magazines regularly featured tailgating recipes, and Helen E. Fleischmann's *Tailgate Cookbook* appeared in 1967. Finger foods, especially submarine sandwiches, crab spread and crackers, relish trays, and brownies, were typical fare. As minivans and SUVs replaced the family station wagon in the 1980s, tailgating evolved into a full-scale operation. Larger vehicle space allowed for complex menus as tailgaters packed up camp stoves, grills, roasters, blenders, and generators to fix meals on site. Grilling, especially, became the most significant element, as more sophisticated tailgating cookbooks tracked with the full-blown tailgating subculture that emerged in the late twentieth- and early twenty-first centuries. As everyman Homer explained in a 2008 episode of *The Simpsons*, "We're not here for the game. The game is nothing. . . . The real reason we Americans put up with sports is for this: Behold, the tailgate party. The pinnacle of human achievement."

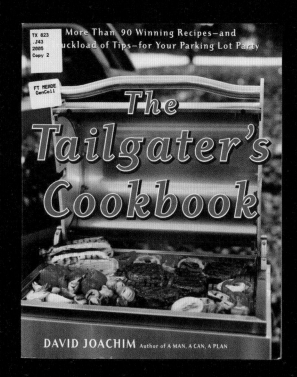

More Than 90 Winning Recipes—and a truckload of Tips—for Your Parking Lot Party

The Tailgater's Cookbook

DAVID JOACHIM Author of A MAN, A CAN, A PLAN

The Tailgater's Cookbook

David Joachim (b. 1967), New York: Broadway Books, 2005. General Collections.

In addition to recipes, this definitive work offers an overview on tailgating traditions, the history of beer, and nuggets of associated trivia. Grilling, however, takes pride of place: "Without a grill, a tailgate is merely a picnic . . . grilling and barbecuing are what make tailgating a uniquely American phenomenon." The recipes reflect that notion, including Tequila Tri-Tip, Beer-Mopped Brisket, and Rum and Cardamom Pork Chops.

Tailgate at Michigan Stadium

Arthur Rothstein (1915–1985), photograph, 1960. LOOK *Magazine Collection, Prints and Photographs Division.*

Prolific photojournalist Arthur Rothstein took this photograph of a Ford Country Squire station wagon hosting a tailgate spread for *LOOK* magazine's October 25, 1960, article "Tail-gate Gourmets." Shot in the legendary "Big House" on the University of Michigan campus, Rothstein's photo illustrated how "the station-wagon set will dine off the deep end of their cars this football season."

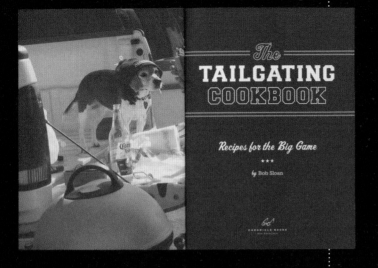

The Tailgating Cookbook:
Recipes for the Big Game

Bob Sloan (b. 1956), San Francisco: Chronicle Books, 2005. General Collections.

"The heart and soul of a tailgate party is the main course," writes the author. "It's what separates the pros from those who tailgate with their backseat stacked with pizzas and subs." The recipes included here emphasize as much at-home preparation as possible, with side dishes (Couscous Salad, Cape Cod Coleslaw, Coconut Rice with Mangoes and Black Beans) ready the day before. Time management is key before kickoff or the green flag: when grilling, allow extra time "to borrow the things you neglected to pack."

Tailgating Done Right:
150 Recipes for a Winning Game Day

Anne Schaeffer. Mount Joy, PA: Fox Chapel Publishing, 2019. General Collections.

The good folks of Cheshire, Massachusetts, are said to have invented the cheese ball; the one they delivered to President Thomas Jefferson in 1801 weighed more than 1,200 pounds. Shortly after World War II, greatly reduced-in-size cheeseballs, often covered in nuts, became a classic American appetizer. An edible modeling clay, cheese shaped into footballs or other relevant objects makes a tailgating favorite fit for a crowd. This cookbook covers the all-day tailgate, with recipes from JumboTron Stud Muffins to Victory Is Ours Margarita Bars.

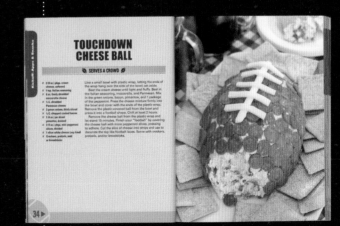

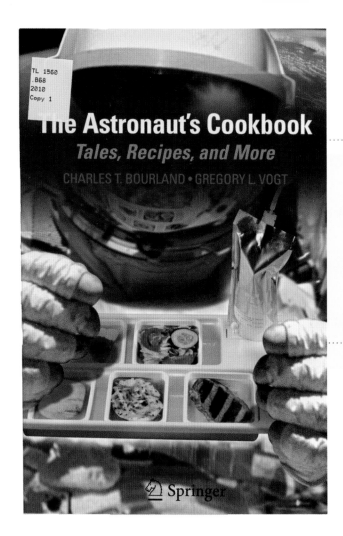

The Astronaut's Cookbook:
Tales, Recipes, and More

 Charles T. Bourland (1937–2019)
and Gregory L. Vogt (b. 1944)

 New York: Springer

 2010

 General Collections

From John Glenn's applesauce-in-a-tube to Apollo 11's cubed sugar cookies to thermostabilized salmon aboard the International Space Station, American space cuisine has taken a giant leap forward in NASA's food laboratories. The no-hassle food prep in microgravity is made possible by the ongoing effort on Earth to develop lightweight, nutritious, and tasty meals that can withstand the rigors of space travel. Although kids have been fixing themselves glasses of Tang—the orange powdered drink mix that accompanied Glenn and other astronauts on their missions—since the 1960s, this cookbook is for those wishing to try more substantial space food without leaving the troposphere. Co-author Charles T. Bourland worked for three decades developing meals and custom packaging for NASA, and the recipes included here can be reproduced at home using ingredients found at the supermarket. Former astronauts also contributed their favorite recipes for meals in orbit, including Col. Gerald Carr's Crock Pot Chili and Dr. Joe Kerwin's Sour Cream Chicken Enchiladas.

A TURKISH BREAKFAST

4 free-range eggs
—
salt and pepper
—
extra-virgin olive oil, for drizzling
—
5 oz feta cheese
—
1–2 tsp dried oregano, or to taste
—
clear honey
—
unsalted butter, softened (for spreading on bread)
—
handful of good black olives
—
2 good-quality sweet Mediterranean tomatoes, sliced
—
Turkish bread
—
black tea

DIFFICULTY: ★ TIME: ★★

Apart from boiling some eggs, there's no cooking involved in creating this Turkish-style breakfast; it's more an assembly of choice ingredients, principally eggs, cheese, olives, tomatoes, bread and honey. Everything is readily available, except perhaps for truly authentic Turkish bread. If you don't have a Turkish grocer nearby, then fresh white bread with sesame seeds will give a reasonable approximation.

Milton's method ☞ Boil the eggs to your liking; hard-boiled is the usual preference with a Turkish breakfast.

If you have hard-boiled your eggs, peel them and cut in quarters, then put on two plates, season with salt and pepper and drizzle a little oil over them.

Cut the feta cheese into slices, arrange on the plates, sprinkle with oregano and drizzle with a little more oil.

Spoon some honey into two small ramekins and put them on the plates. Do the same with some softened butter.

Arrange the olives and the tomatoes on the plates and serve with the bread and some light, slightly sweetened black tea.

95

The Hungover Cookbook

 Milton Crawford

 New York: Clarkson Potter

 2011

 General Collections

Milton Crawford's book opens with puzzles to help determine the reader's level of hangover, followed by recipes that avoid the clichéd "hair of the dog" remedies. Dishes include Elvis Presley's famous banana bacon peanut butter sandwich; kedgeree, an Indian egg and fish dish; cardamom porridge; and this one for a Turkish Breakfast that involves little actual cooking—helpful if you're too hungover to cook safely. Perhaps out of order, Crawford wrote a sequel in 2014 titled *The Drunken Cookbook*.

Food Truck Road Trip:
A Cookbook

 Kim Pham and Philip Shen
with Terri Phillips

 Salem, MA: Page Street Publishing

 2014

 General Collections

In mobile food service history, street-corner carts, military field kitchens, Oscar Mayer Weiner Mobiles, and xylophone-music-playing ice cream trucks paved the road for souped-up food trucks that frequent sidewalks and festivals. During the 2010s, the number of food trucks in the United States nearly doubled as entrepreneurial chefs put their message on social media and took their specialties to the streets, offering everything from classic comfort food to fusion dishes on paper plates. In search of the best food truck food and their recipes, the authors embarked on an All-American cross-country adventure from the West Coast (Roast Beef with Béchamel Cheese Sauce/Big-Ass Sandwiches, Portland), around the Deep South (Grilled Chicken Cordon Bleu Sliders/NOLA Girl Food Truck, New Orleans), to I-95 (Watermelon Gazpacho/Deli-icious, Raleigh). In a cookbook that also showcases chef tales and extensive photography, the authors document yet another American tradition that compulsively combines good eats and a preoccupation with motor vehicles (see pages 124 and 133).

The Sioux Chef's Indigenous Kitchen

In 2014, Sean Sherman, Oglala Lakota, created The Sioux Chef, a catering and food education business. The organization, and the cookbook he wrote three years later, focuses on the revitalization and awareness of indigenous foods systems. Recipes—such as maple-juniper roast pheasant; rabbit braised with apples and mint; and grilled bison skewers with *wojape*, a berry sauce—avoid traditional European ingredients like wheat, dairy, and processed sugar, and instead focus on game, fish, berries, and native plants. The book won the prestigious James Beard award in 2018 for best American cookbook. Four years later Owamni, a full-service indigenous-cuisine restaurant in Minneapolis run by the Sioux Chef, also won a Beard award, for Best New Restaurant in America.

 Sean Sherman (b. 1974) with Beth Dooley (b. 1954)

 Minneapolis: University of Minnesota Press

 2017

 General Collections

THE
SI◆UX CHEF'S
INDIGENOUS KITCHEN

SEAN SHERMAN
WITH BETH DOOLEY

University of Minnesota Press
Minneapolis
London

The Taco Tuesday Cookbook: *52 Tasty Taco Recipes to Make Every Week the Best Ever*

Laura Fuentes

Beverly, MA: Fair Winds Press

2018

General Collections

Tuesday as taco day has a history that dates back at least to 1933, when the White Star Cafeteria in El Paso, Texas, promoted the weekly occasion. A regular feature on outdoor chalkboards, if not a national institution, "Taco Tuesday" is celebrated coast-to-coast: as early as 1971, El Charro on Route 44 in Avon, Connecticut, was featuring the phrase in its advertisements. Recognizing tacos' alliterative and critical place on the calendar, this cookbook showcases a year's worth of weekly taco variations photographed tostada-style for improved visual effect. Recipes cover breakfast, vegetarian, meat, and seafood tacos that sample both classic and fusion approaches, such as Jamaican jerk chicken, Thai ribs, Hawaiian pork, and Cajun shrimp fillings. As part of her research, the author consumed tacos at least once—and often thrice—weekly, for about two years. "There's something about having a vessel like a tortilla to hold together all of the decadent flavors of a taco filling—and of course the accompaniments and the sauces drizzled on top. It's the whole package," she writes, pinpointing why tacos are regarded as a fun food.

Whimsical Elephant (with Martini Glass) *on the Illinois State Fairgrounds in Springfield, Illinois*

 Carol M. Highsmith (b. 1946)

 Digital photograph

 2019

 Prints and Photographs Division

A Martini-drinking pachyderm and roadside attraction, Pinky, as he is inevitably called, has been Springfield's most social celebrity since 1972, appearing at the state fair, innumerable parades and parties, and at least one funeral procession. He's been abducted, blown over, and inadvertently sliced in half, but always returns, glass in trunk, for the next event.

Cacao, the plant from which chocolate is made, was first cultivated by the ancient Mayans. Their preferred method of consumption for chocolate was as a thick, bitter, frothy drink served cold. I prefer to make a chocolate syrup that is thick; adding a bit of spice and smoke transports it to another place, how I imagine the Yucatán to taste and feel. • **MAKES 1**

MAYAN CAMPFIRE

2 OUNCES **123 ORGANIC REPOSADO (DOS) TEQUILA**

2 OUNCES **CHOCOLATE SYRUP** (RECIPE FOLLOWS)

1 BARSPOON **SMOKED JALAPEÑO TEQUILA** (RECIPE FOLLOWS)

5 OR 6 **MARSHMALLOWS** (RECIPE FOLLOWS), FOR GARNISH

In a cocktail shaker, combine the tequila, chocolate syrup, and smoked jalapeño tequila with ice. Shake, then strain into a rocks glass filled with ice. Place the marshmallows on top and slowly toast them with a small kitchen torch (see Sources, page 153). Be very careful not to apply the flame for too long on any one area near the rim of the glass. The whole process should take less than 10 seconds.

 Matthew Biancaniello (b. 1968)

 New York: Dey St.

 2016

 General Collections

Eat Your Drink: *Culinary Cocktails*

Matthew Biancaniello served as the "cocktail chef" at the former Library Bar in the famous Hollywood Roosevelt Hotel in Los Angeles. He is known for creating cocktails that use local and sustainable produce to make what he calls "farm-to-glass" concoctions, ranging from amuse-bouche cocktails (a cherry tomato-infused with tequila) to dessert drinks like the pictured Mayan Campfire. Inspired by the Mayans' cultivation of the cacao plant, the drink combines jalapeño tequila, chocolate, and torched marshmallow in a sweet-and-spicy toast to the Yucatán that harkens back to the original cocktail recipe of spirits, sugar, water, and bitters.

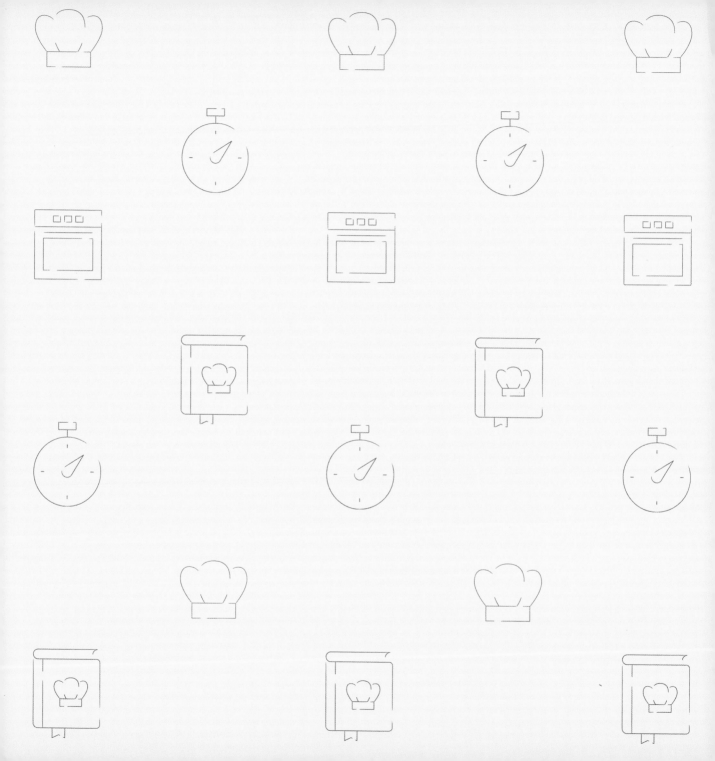

Acknowledgements

This book is dedicated to Connie Carter, former Head of the Science Reference Section, Science, Technology, and Business Division, Library of Congress. Thank you for your guidance, expertise, and delicious chocolate chip cookies.

Text by Zach Klitzman and Susan Reyburn, with contributions from Becky Clark.

Design by Jessica Epting.

The authors gratefully acknowledge the assistance and scholarship of their Library of Congress colleagues: JJ Harbster, Alison Kelly (ret.), and Connie Carter (ret.) (Science, Technology, and Business Division); Bruce Kirby, Michelle Krowl, Josh Levy, Meg McAleer, and Liz Novara (Manuscript Division); Megan Harris and Nathan Cross (Veterans History Project); Mark Dimunation, Michael North, and Amanda Zimmerman (Rare Book and Special Collections Division); Cheryl Regan (Exhibits Office); Paul Sommerfeld and Libby Smigel (Music Division); Josie Walters-Johnston (Motion Picture, Broadcast, and Recorded Sound Division); Gary Johnson (Newspaper and Current Periodical Division); Domenic Sergi and Andrew Cook (Digital Scan Center); David Mandel (Center for Exhibitions & Interpretation); Mike Munshaw and Jessica Epting (Design Office); Becky Clark, Pete Devereaux, Hannah Freece, Aimee Hess, Porsha Perry; interns Samantha Baine, Jane Brinley, Polina Lopez, Juliet Machado, and Jude Souazoube (Publishing Office).

All items come from Library of Congress collections.

Unless otherwise noted, all cookbooks featured are first editions.

Life dates in captions are included where known.

Further Reading

Links to Library of Congress Resources:

- Food & Nutrition Research Guide: https://guides.loc.gov/food-nutrition
- Katherine Golden Bitting Collection: https://www.loc.gov/rr/rarebook/coll/028.html
- Online Presentation of Community Cookbooks: https://guides.loc.gov/community-cookbooks
- Research Guide on Presidential Food: https://guides.loc.gov/presidential-food
- Research Guide on Early Mixology Books: https://guides.loc.gov/early-mixology-books
- Food, Foodways, and Food History Webcasts:
- https://guides.loc.gov/science-webcasts/subject_food_history
- Henrietta Nesbitt Papers: https://hdl.loc.gov/loc.mss/eadmss.ms013053
- Veterans History Project: https://www.loc.gov/vets/

Selected Secondary Sources:

- Bower, Anne L., editor. *Recipes for Reading: Community Cookbooks, Stories, Histories*. Amherst: University of Massachusetts Press, 1997.
- Brown, Derek with Robert Yule. *Spirits, Sugar, Water, Bitters: How the Cocktail Conquered the World*. New York: Rizzoli, 2018.
- Charming, Cheryl. *The Cocktail Companion: A Guide to Cocktail History, Culture, Trivia and Favorite Drinks*. Coral Gables, FL: Mango Publishing Group, 2018.
- Fisher, Carol. *The American Cookbook: A History*. Jefferson, NC: McFarland, 2006.
- Haber, Barbara. *From Hardtack to Home Fries: an Uncommon History of American Cooks and Meals*. New York: Free Press, 2002.
- Neuhaus, Jessamyn. *Manly Meals and Mom's Home Cooking: Cookbooks and Gender in Modern America*. Baltimore: The Johns Hopkins University Press, 2003.
- Notaker, Henry. *A History of Cookbooks: From Kitchen to Page over Seven Centuries*. Oakland: University of California Press, 2017.
- Schenone, Laura. *A Thousand Years over a Hot Stove: A History of American Women Told through Food, Recipes, and Remembrances*. New York: W. W. Norton, 2003.
- Schremp, Gerry. *Celebration of American Food: Four Centuries in the Melting Pot*. Golden, CO: Fulcrum Press in cooperation with the Library of Congress, 1996.
- Stavely, Keith and Kathleen Fitzgerald. *United Tastes: The Making of the First American Cookbook*. Amherst: University of Massachusetts Press, 2017.
- Tipton-Martin, Toni. *The Jemima Code: Two Centuries of African American Cookbooks*. Austin: University of Texas Press, 2015.
- Wondrich, David. *Imbibe! From Absinthe Cocktail to Whiskey Smash, a Salute in Stories and Drinks to "Professor" Jerry Thomas, Pioneer of the American Bar*. New York: Perigee, 2007.

Credits

Images from Prints and Photographs Division

The images listed below are from the Prints and Photographs Division and include an identification number; these items can be located by searching for that number at www.loc.gov/pictures.

Frontispiece: LC-DIG-ppmsca-45486

16: LC-DIG-pga-02298

42: LC-DIG-ppmsca-28084

44: LC-DIG-fsa-8b07826

46: LC-USZ62-123257

57: LC-USZC2-5150

62: LC-USZC2-5203

92: LC-DIG-ppmsca-59315

110: LC-DIG-hlb-10946

119: LC-DIG-ppmsca-09899

126: LC-DIG-vrg-13205

131: LC-DIG-ppmsca-54111

134: LC-DIG-ds-03644

141: LC-DIG-highsm-59303

Chapters 1 and 2

All items and images in chapters 1 and 2 are in the public domain

Chapter 3

- 52, 53: From Scribner Permissions - Joy of Cooking materials. Copyright © New York: Scribner, 2022. Reprinted with the permission of Scribner, a division of Simon & Schuster, Inc. All rights reserved.
- 55: Courtesy of Mrs. Thomas Cobb Brody
- 58, 59: Courtesy of Family of Henrietta Nesbitt
- 59 (right): Permission from the Estate of Eleanor Roosevelt
- 63: Courtesy of Literary Trust u/w/o M.F.K. Fisher
- 68: Courtesy of Ken and Maggie Schacht

Chapter 4

- 72: Illustrations from THE FINE ART OF MIXING DRINKS by David A. Embury, copyright © 1952, 1958, renewed © 1980, 1986 by Ruth A. Embury & Margaret Embury Demange. Used by permission of Random House, an imprint and division of Penguin Random House LLC. All rights reserved.
- 73: Courtesy of Buwei Yang Chao Estate
- 74: Used by permission of G. Schirmer, Inc.
- 77 (left): Courtesy of White Rock Products Corp.
- 77 (right), 79: Courtesy of the Sazerac Company Archives at Buffalo Trace Distillery – Frankfort, KY
- 78 (left): Courtesy of Diageo
- 78 (right): Courtesy of Pernod-Ricard USA
- 80: Betty Crocker is a registered trademark of General Mills. © General Mills.
- 82: Courtesy of the Rosa and Raymond Parks Institute for Self Development
- 83: Recipe for Haschich Fudge from *The Alice B. Toklas Cook Book* by Alice B. Toklas. Copyright 1954 by Alice B. Toklas. Copyright renewed 1982 by Edward M. Burns. Used by permission of HarperCollins Publishers.
- 85 (top): Courtesy of Leita Voss Hamill
- 86: Courtesy of Naval Institute Press
- 87: Courtesy of Hearst Magazine Media, Inc.
- 88: Courtesy of Reed College
- 89: Courtesy of Favorite Recipes Press, Southwestern Publishing House
- 90: "Boeuf Bourguignon" from MASTERING THE ART OF FRENCH COOKING, VOLUME 1 by Julia Child, Louisette Bertholle, and Simone Beck, copyright © 1961 by Alfred A. Knopf, a division of Penguin Random House LLC. Used by permission of Alfred A. Knopf, an imprint of the Knopf Doubleday Publishing Group, a division of Penguin Random House LLC. All rights reserved.

- 91 (left): Courtesy of Jinx Kragen Morgan and Judy Perry
- 91 (right): Courtesy of Alice Baer
- 92: Courtesy of Jane Oka
- 95 (bottom): From MAN WITH A PAN by John Donahue © 2011 by John Donahue. Reprinted by Permission of Algonquin Books of Chapel Hill. All rights reserved.

Chapter 5

- 96: Courtesy of Renée Comet @Cometphoto.com
- 99: Courtesy of Victor Hazan
- 100: Julie Eisenhower's Cookbook for Children cover (c) SEPS licensed by Curtis Licensing, Indianapolis, IN. All rights reserved.
- 101: Courtesy of Favorite Recipes Press, Southwestern Publishing House
- 102: Copyright © 1976, 2004 by George H. Schiters; first appeared in *To Serve Man: A Cookbook for People* under the byline Karl Wurf; reprinted by permission of Wildeside Press and The Virginia Kidd Agency, Inc.
- 103: From the estate of Irene Kuo
- 104: Courtesy of anonymous
- 105: Courtesy of Donovan Jon Fandre
- 106: Courtesy of Simon and Schuster
- 107: Photo copyright Kathryn Kleinman © 1981
- 108: Excerpted from *Entertaining*, by Martha Stewart. Photographs (from left) by Michael Skott and Richard Jeffrey. Copyright ©1982 by Martha Stewart. Reprinted by permission of Clarkson Potter/Publishers, an imprint of Random House, a division of Penguin Random House LLC.
- 110: A 1984 Herblock Cartoon, © The Herb Block Foundation
- 111: *Elegant Wine Cocktails*, Published by Directed Media, Inc.
- 113: © 1988 Touchstone Pictures Photo: Richard Corman
- 114 (left): Courtesy of Universal Studios Licensing LLC
- 114 (right): Licensed By: Warner Bros. Entertainment Inc. All Rights Reserved
- 116: Courtesy of Kensington Publishing Corp
- 118: Leah Chase, *The Dooky Chase Cookbook* (New Orleans: Pelican Publishing, 1990). Used by permission of Pelican Publishing. All rights reserved.
- 119 and cover: Courtesy of Carmen Lomas Garza
- 120: Courtesy of the National Council of Negro Women
- 122: Courtesy of Joan Nathan, Cookbook Author
- 123: Illustrations and "Recipes for the Chef: Hors D'oeuvres" from SEAGRAM'S NEW OFFICIAL BARTENDER'S GUIDE by Affinity Publishing, copyright © 1995 by Affinity Communications Corp. Used by permission of Viking Books, an imprint of Penguin Publishing Group, a division of Penguin Random House LLC. All rights reserved.
- 125 (top): Courtesy of Chris Maynard and Bill Scheller

Chapter 6

- 126: Courtesy of Camilo Jose Vergara
- 128: Cover of *The Easy Bake Oven Gourmet* by David Hoffman, copyright © 2003. Reprinted by permission of Running Press, an imprint of Hachette Book Group, Inc.
- 129: Courtesy of Meredith Licensing
- 130: Courtesy of Jay Coldren
- 131: Courtesy of Maira Kalman and Rick Meyerowitz
- 132: Courtesy of Fair Winds Press
- 135 (right): *Tailgating Done Right Cookbook* © 2019 by Anne Schaeffer and Fox Chapel Publishing, recipe and photograph by Rada Mfg DBA CQ Products.
- 136: Charles T. Bourland and Gregory L. Vogt, *The Astronaut's Cookbook*, published 2010, Springer Science + Business Media, reproduced with permission of Springer Nature, permission conveyed through Copyright Clearance Center, Inc.
- 137: "A Turkish Breakfast" from THE HUNGOVER COOKBOOK by Milton Crawford, copyright © 2010 by Milton Crawford. Used by permission of Clarkson Potter/Publishers, an imprint of Random House, a division of Penguin Random House LLC. All rights reserved.
- 138: Originally published by Page Street Publishing
- 139: *The Sioux Chef's Indigenous Kitchen* by Sean Sherman with Beth Dooley. Published by the University of Minnesota Press, 2017. Copyright 2017 Ghost Dancer, Inc. Frontispiece photograph by Nancy Bundt. Used by permission.
- 140: Courtesy of Fair Winds Press
- 142: "Mayan Campfire" from *Eat Your Drink* by Matthew Biancaniello. Copyright (c) 2016 by Matthew Biancaniello. Used by permission of HarperCollins Publishers.

Index